The Two Henrys

Henry Plant and Henry Flagler and Their Railroads

Sandra Wallus Sammons

Pineapple Press, Inc.
Sarasota, Florida

To Tawny Faye Sammons, a grand granddaughter

Inquiries should be addressed to:

Pineapple Press, Inc.
P.O. Box 3889
Sarasota, Florida 34230

www.pineapplepress.com

Library of Congress Cataloging-in-Publication Data

Sammons, Sandra Wallus.
The two Henrys : Henry Plant and Henry Flagler and their railroads /
Sandra Wallus Sammons. -- 1st ed.
   p. cm.
Includes bibliographical references and index.
ISBN 978-1-56164-456-8 (hbk. : alk. paper) -- ISBN 978-1-56164-461-
2 (pbk. : alk. paper)
1. Plant, Henry Bradley, 1819-1899. 2. Flagler, Henry Morrison,
1830-1913. 3. Railroads--Florida--History. 4. Industrialists--Florida--
Biography. I. Title.
HE2752.S36 2010
385.092'2759--dc22

                        2010002212

First Edition
Hb: 10 9 8 7 6 5 4 3 2 1
Pb: 10 9 8 7 6 5 4 3 2

Design by Shé Hicks
Printed in the United States of America

Contents

Acknowledgments

Thanks to John M. Blades, Executive Director of the Flagler Museum, Palm Beach; David Carson, Public Affairs Director at the Flagler Museum; Amanda Wilson, Public Affairs Department Assistant at the Flagler Museum; Susan Carter, Curator/Registrar at the Henry B. Plant Museum, Tampa; Gianna Russo, Curator of Education, Henry B. Plant Museum; Seth H. Bramson, Company Historian, Florida East Coast Railway, Adjunct Professor of History at Barry University and Florida International University (both in Miami), and author of fourteen books on south Florida local and Florida transportation history; Thomas Graham, Professor of History Emeritus, Flagler College, St. Augustine; Dan Gallagher, author of *Florida's Great Ocean Railway: Building the Key West Extension*; Donna Dunakey, Curriculum and Instruction Specialist, Social Sciences PK-12, Charlotte County Public Schools; Susan James, Gifted Teacher, L. A. Ainger Middle School, Charlotte County Public Schools; L. A. Ainger Middle School students Miranda Bergeron and Owen D. Berry; Janis Russell, Reference & Adult Services Librarian, North Port Library; and Phyllis Lewis, Elizabeth and Richard (Railfan) Poole, and Bob Sammons for reading the manuscript. Thanks also to Mark Knox, seventh grade teacher and Social Studies Department Chairman at L. A. Ainger Middle School, and to the librarians in the Sarasota County Library System, particularly at the Elsie Quirk Library in Englewood, for their great help with my many inter-library loan requests.

A special thank-you as well to my publisher, Pineapple Press, for encouraging my writing about Florida's exciting history, and to Heather Waters, for her editorial assistance.

Foreword

Years ago, wagons pulled by horses slipped in mud or stuck in sand. Wooden rails placed under wagon wheels were found to make hauling easier. Iron straps on the tops of the rails made the ride smoother. Flanged, or grooved, wheels allowed a better grip on the track. Iron rails were even sturdier and safer. Step by step, the railroad as we know it today was born.

The steam engine was invented, and steamboats made transportation faster and more dependable. The railroad came of age when steam was harnessed to power a locomotive running on those iron rails, and when horse power was replaced by the "iron horse."

Just when the railroad was ready for the country, America, bursting with growth, was ready for the railroad. Railroads helped business, and they became big business too. Rails even united the nation in 1869 with a trans-continental railway connecting the Atlantic Ocean to the Pacific. The history of American railroading is a fascinating story, filled with creativity and innovative ideas, all happening while some on the sidelines said, "That's impossible!"

Our focus will be on the growth of Florida's railroads, and two Henrys who changed the state with their own creativity, innovation, and money. Henry Plant and Henry Flagler were the forces behind changes to laws and the clearing of land to fill a public need, even as they endured losses in their personal lives. Both ignored the word "impossible," and when they were finished, Florida had a thriving economy and had become an "American Riviera."

And the two Henrys had fun doing it.

Chapter 1

Young Florida

The buzzing of dozens of mosquitoes. The snapping sounds of
alligator jaws as the reptiles feasted on hundreds of fish in the lakes
and rivers. The screeching of thousands of birds landing on millions
of trees. Those were the sounds of early Florida.

Previously claimed by Spain, Florida became a territory of the
United States in 1821. Indian villages dotted the peninsula, and when
settlers came from Northern states, they built forts in the wilderness
to keep the Indians away. Fort Brooke at Tampa Bay, Fort Dallas on
the Miami River, and other forts and camps grew slowly into small
towns. Some villages grew because of their location on waterways.
Roads between the small settlements were either bad or did not exist
at all.

The hardy few who came and stayed were rewarded with
abundant harvests from field and forest. Citrus and cotton grew well,
and lumber was plentiful. By 1827, steamboats plying Florida's
waterways helped distribute some of the wealth, but horses and
wagons were still needed between farm and boat. Faster and more

dependable land transportation was needed. Railroads, already spreading through Northern states, were the answer.

By 1837, Richard Keith Call, later governor of the territory, completed one of Florida's first railroads. His twenty-three-mile-long Tallahassee Railroad carried cotton from the fields of the capital area to St. Marks on the Gulf of Mexico. The "railroad" track was primitive, made of wood topped with iron straps. The small wooden cars were pulled by mules at first.

When Florida became the twenty-seventh state in the United States on March 3, 1845, miles of wilderness land were available for economic development. In 1855 the Internal Improvement Fund Act was passed to oversee the proper distribution of lands. The land was to be used for farming, industry, development of towns, and railroads. If someone wanted to build a railroad, he would have to request a "charter." If approved, the charter holder would receive land for every mile of track laid. A charter also gave the right to "bonds," or state government loans for the purchase of needed equipment.

These incentives, or bonuses meant to encourage development, were intriguing for many. One of Florida's first U. S. senators, David Levy Yulee, was given a charter for a much-needed cross-Florida railroad. He had permission to link Fernandina Beach on the east

⚙ When he tried to modernize his line, Call experienced the frustration of all early railroad owners. He bought two of the latest steam locomotives, but one boiler exploded and the second slid off the unsteady tracks—right into the St. Marks River. He explained to his friends: "We have taken the locomotives off the road, and intend never to use them again. We find horse power superior."

A horse-drawn railroad car traveling along the St. Johns Railway, which ran from Tocoi to St. Augustine. 1874. (Courtesy of the State Archives of Florida)

coast with Cedar Key on the west coast by rail. This would eliminate the need for passengers and freight to travel by steamship around Florida's peninsula and through the dangerous Florida Straits south of Key West. Yulee's Florida Railroad was completed in 1861.

The St. Johns Railway, another early railroad, was chartered in 1858. It connected St. Augustine, an important city in the days when Spain owned Florida, to the St. Johns River. With no good roads into the historic city, it was difficult to reach, and St. Augustine had become a neglected city.

From 1861 to 1865, the devastating Civil War stopped most construction in Florida, and much of the existing track was either

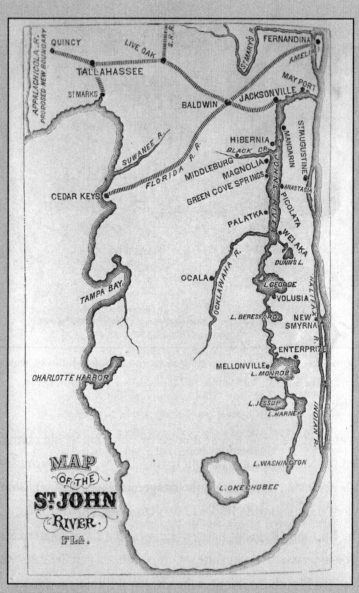

A drawing of the St. Johns River. This map also shows some of the early railroads in Florida. Exact date unknown. (Courtesy of the State Archives of Florida)

damaged or destroyed.

Although reconstruction after the war was slow in the South, progress was made. On May 10, 1869, the first continuous, transcontinental line of railroad track actually crossed America. All of America was opened up for settlement, and Florida felt the surge. The state's population soared as adventurers encouraged friends to come south, probably not telling them the truth about the number of mosquitoes and alligators they had seen. Many came because the sunshine and warmth were good for their health, and many stayed because they appreciated the beauty and the bounty of the place.

Yulee's cross-state Florida Railroad (later called the Florida Transit Railroad) patched up its badly damaged track. Colonel William Dudley Chipley received a charter to build from Pensacola eastward to the Apalachicola River, encouraging the growth of towns in Florida's Panhandle. Northern millionaire William Astor, owner of the St. Johns Railway to St. Augustine, built an extension that took his railway's track farther south, to Palatka.

Franklin W. Smith of Massachusetts bought land on King Street in St. Augustine and built the Villa Zorayda, one of the first all-concrete homes in America, in the Moorish, or Middle Eastern, style popular at the time. Harriet Beecher Stowe, author of *Uncle Tom's Cabin*, came from New England to spend time in Mandarin, on the banks of the beautiful St. Johns River. Stowe gave Florida tourism a boost when her book, *Palmetto Leaves*, was published in 1873. In it, she described Florida as a paradise:

> If you want to see a new and peculiar beauty, watch
> a golden sunset through a grove draperied with gray
> moss. The swaying, filmy bands turn golden and rose-

colored; and the long, swaying avenues are like a
scene in fairyland.

Henry S. Sanford, a former ambassador to Belgium, bought land
along the shores of Lake Monroe, planted orange groves, built the
Sanford House Hotel, and started a town called Sanford. Hamilton
Disston of Philadelphia, a friend of Sanford's, didn't start a town, but
he bought and attempted to drain land in the Everglades. The money
from his purchase allowed Florida's government to spend money again
on encouraging railroad development in the state.

The timing was perfect. Two creative Northern businessmen with
money to spare, Henry Bradley Plant and Henry Morrison Flagler,
were just getting familiar with Florida. Henry Plant wanted to expand
his business throughout the Southern states, and Henry Flagler needed
a new project after making millions in Standard Oil. There were risks
involved, but oh, what a great challenge!

Florida was ripe for development, and two Henrys were coming.

Chapter 2

Young Henry Plant

Henry Bradley Plant was born in Branford, Connecticut, on October 27, 1819. He lived with his family until he finished the eighth grade in school. Then he took a job where he could be outdoors and see something of the world.

He was hired as a captain's boy on one of the new steamboats carrying passengers and freight across the waters of Long Island Sound. As the boat made its way between New Haven and New York City, young Plant kept the decks clean. Living aboard the boat, he ate his meals standing up in the galley and slept downstairs in a small, crowded room. He saved every penny he could for a more comfortable future.

America was expanding quickly, and the United States Postal Service was growing with it. However, privately owned express-freight companies—early versions of today's FedEx and UPS—were also getting into the business. Henry Plant would learn that business from the ground up, and his careful attention to his duties earned him great respect and quick promotions. When the boat captain created a separate room designated for packages, Henry Plant was

Henry Bradley Plant at approximately thirty-six years of age. He is dressed for work at Adams Express Company. 1855. (Collection of Gregg M. Turner)

put in charge. He gratefully accepted the job, knowing that he would have his own bed in the freight room!

At age twenty-two, he put his days on the steamboat behind him when he married Miss Ellen Elizabeth Blackstone. Plant decided to continue working in the business of package shipment by accepting an office position with a New Haven express firm, Beecher & Company. Quickly rising through the ranks, he was asked to move to the company's New York office. Henry and Ellen Plant were happy in the growing city, but soon after the birth of their second child, Morton Freeman Plant, Ellen became sick. Two doctors agreed that she had congestion of the lungs and that cold northern winters were making her cough worse.

America in the 1850s had more than twenty thousand miles of railroad track, but many of them did not connect. To travel from New York to Florida, it was still easier to go south by steamship. Plant could afford the best accommodations, but even the best meant a long and tiring journey.

In March of 1853, Mr. and Mrs. Plant boarded the steamship

Marion for the trip from New York City to Charleston, South
Carolina. Then the *Calhoun* took them on to Savannah, Georgia, and
the *Welaka* finally steamed into the harbor at Jacksonville, completing
their eight-day trip. After staying one night in that small town, they
crossed to the south side of the St. Johns River in a dugout canoe, a
boat used by the early Florida Indians.

Staying at a settler's home in Strawberry Mills, the Plants enjoyed
the peacefulness of their surroundings and the warm weather, both
of which brought back Ellen's health. Interested in seeing nearby St.
Augustine, Plant suggested a short visit there. They took a horse and
buggy along the Old King's Road, twenty miles filled with ruts and
bumps and mosquitoes. Despite the uncomfortable ride, both enjoyed
the charm of the historic town. After about six weeks, Plant made
sure that Ellen would remain comfortable for another two months
in Florida and then returned to New York by himself. His trip back
North was likely filled with thoughts of the beauty of the flowers, the
relaxing lifestyle, and the hospitality of the people he had met. Florida
had made a favorable impression on Henry Plant.

Realizing that his wife would be healthier if they lived in a
warmer climate, Plant made business arrangements to work for
Adams Express Company in Augusta, Georgia. Plant became
superintendent of the Southern department, in charge of all of Adams'
growth in the South.

In those days before e-mail or fax machines, the superintendent
of the Southern division had to travel extensively to encourage the

⚙ Early short-line train rides were not very relaxing. Passenger
cars got hot and stuffy with the windows closed. But if you
opened the windows, soot and cinders from the engine flew in.

⚙ The bumpy Old King's Road was built between 1763 and 1783, when England had ownership of Florida by a treaty with Spain. It ran south from the St. Marys River through Cow Ford (now Jacksonville). Then it went on to St. Augustine on its way to New Smyrna.

growth of the smaller offices. Plant took any means of transportation available to him. He traveled on unreliable steamboats, bumpy stagecoaches, and short railroads. This was a great time of learning for Henry Plant. He added to his knowledge of the express business, and he learned about the need for a connected transportation system in the Southern states.

Modern, connecting railroads were spreading throughout the North, and Plant met many entrepreneurs starting railroads in the Southern states too. He heard stories of successes and failures, and learned from both. Plant's long hours on the road were well spent. Adams Express grew quickly, and he became one of the best-known men in the South. Plant and his wife spent some time during winters in Florida together. They explored different areas of the undeveloped state, always returning with a great appreciation for the beauty and warmth there.

By 1860, however, a Civil War was about to erupt in America.

The next year, 1861, brought two major changes to Henry Plant's life. The first occurred when winter brought unusually cold weather even to Georgia and Ellen's cough returned. Plant was notified and returned home immediately, but this time his wife did not recover. Ellen Plant died on February 28, 1861, at forty years of age. Henry Plant was heartbroken.

The second major change was with his position at Adams

Express. Alvin Adams, the owner of the company, witnessed in person the bombing at Fort Sumter on April 12, 1861, that began the Civil War. He began to fear that that his Northern-based company would not survive the conflict. Adams' problem was Henry Plant's opportunity.

Although born in the North himself, Plant bought the Southern part of the business. He incorporated his new Southern Express Company in the state of Georgia. He sent his lawyer immediately to inform Confederate President Jefferson Davis that Southern Express was a Georgia company. Davis was told that Plant believed the war to be a mistake, but that if there had to be a conflict, his well-established and efficient shipping business could be very helpful to the Southern war effort.

Davis liked Plant's honesty. He granted him Confederate citizenship and accepted the ready help with moving packages and supplies for the soldiers. Realizing the responsibility he then had, Plant worked even more hours, hoping also to escape his grief at losing Ellen. Soon totally exhausted, he was told by his doctors that he needed a total rest. Plant sailed for Europe, trying to put thoughts of war and grief behind him, but still very aware that life would be quite different on his return.

Chapter 3

Henry Plant's First Railroads

By the time Henry Plant returned from Europe, he was anxious to get back to work. The Civil War ended in 1865, and Southern Express had prospered.

The late 1800s were an exciting, vibrant time in America, and limitations were pushed aside. A railroad reached from the Atlantic to the Pacific, and there was talk of a canal between the oceans, somewhere in Central America. Joseph F. Monier patented a reinforced concrete process, making possible the construction of stronger bridges. John A. Roebling built the Brooklyn Bridge in New York. Alexander Graham Bell invented the telephone. Thomas Alva Edison and J. W. Swan devised the first practical electric light. It was a time of many inventions and many profits, and America entered a "gilded age."

Plant took time out from his thriving business to marry Margaret Josephine Loughman on July 2, 1873, twelve years after the death of his first wife. Following a honeymoon trip to Europe, they returned home to Augusta, Georgia, and later moved to a new home on Fifth Avenue in New York City.

Henry Plant had been in the express business for almost forty years, and it was a natural extension of that career to invest in railroads. Northern railroads were growing into great railroad systems, and Plant knew that, to work efficiently, many small Southern railroads needed expertise and money. He decided to invest primarily in lines in the South.

In 1879, Plant became the owner of a railroad. The Atlantic & Gulf Railroad had great potential to be an important line in the South, but it was having financial problems. It connected Savannah on the Atlantic with Bainbridge on the Flint River, a 237-mile route across southern Georgia. Two existing branches off the main line also interested Plant, since one went north to the rich agricultural lands at Albany, Georgia, and one went south to Live Oak, in Florida. A further bonus of owning the A&G was its excellent superintendent, Colonel Henry S. Haines of Savannah, Georgia. He had been in charge of Confederate railroads in the Carolinas during the Civil War.

Along with the railroad track, Plant also bought steam engines and railway cars. Henry Plant was starting a new career—as owner of what would become the mighty Plant System of Railways.

He changed the name of the A & G railroad to the Savannah, Florida & Western Railway, making the path of his new venture quite clear. Track on the SF&W was changed to standard gauge, passenger car interiors were re-modeled for greater comfort, and new equipment led to greater efficiency. Colonel Henry Haines stayed on as general manager, with his main office in Savannah. Henry Plant was president of the SF&W, with his office in New York City.

Obviously Plant already had a plan. His second acquisition took place less than a year later, again with the backing and advice of wealthy friends. Plant bought the Savannah & Charleston Railroad,

⊛ In 1861, eight changes of train were necessary for a trip
between Charleston, South Carolina, and Philadelphia,
Pennsylvania, because of the differences in track. Some track
was built with the rails closer together, called narrow gauge,
and some with the rails farther apart, called wide gauge. Later,
a standardized gauge for track allowed for complete trips on
one train.

which created a smoother flow between those two important cotton-
exporting ports. It also formed a through track from Charleston, South
Carolina, to Bainbridge in western Georgia, and then to Florida. Rather
than include it in the Savannah, Florida & Western, however, Plant
simply changed the name to the Charleston & Savannah Railway.

These two railroads, separate in name but continuous in track,
were the backbone of Plant's expansion throughout the South. His
timing was perfect. During the decade of the 1880s, a record amount
of about seventy-five thousand miles of new railroad track was built
in America. And in 1881 the Florida state government, through the
Internal Improvement Fund, again started giving away large grants of
land for new railroad track to be built. Henry Plant, who already had
one foot in Florida at Live Oak, was ready.

There was, however, no welcome mat at Florida's border.
Too many greedy people, known as "carpetbaggers," had already
come south after the Civil War just to take advantage of the area's
devastation. Plant had to tactfully convince the Southerners that *his*
only goal was to create a better railroad system for all. Clearly better

transportation was needed. G. W. Nichols wrote in *Harper's Magazine* in October 1870: "There are two ways of getting to Jacksonville from Savannah, and whichever you choose, you will be sorry you had not taken the other."

Before 1881 the only rail link between Savannah and Jacksonville, both on the Atlantic Ocean, went inland to Lawton (later Dupont) in Georgia, south to Live Oak in Florida, then east again to Jacksonville. Plant obtained a Georgia charter to build southeast from Waycross. He got a separate charter from Florida to build northwest from Jacksonville. A railroad bridge across the St. Marys River was built between the two, and the "Waycross Short Line" cut travel time in half for those traveling from Jacksonville to Savannah. Travelers were grateful, and Plant now had a second entrance into Florida.

With two feet firmly planted in the state, Plant was making it possible for Floridians to reach the rest of America and for the rest of Americans to reach Florida more easily. Jacksonville, long isolated, was now starting to grow as a port city and as a terminus for trains. Although the trip from New York still took thirty-six hours, passengers could finally ride in comfort on one train all the way. When refrigerated freight cars, cooled by ice, were added, even Florida's fruits, vegetables, and fresh fish could ride in comfort to Northern markets!

By this time Henry Plant was in his early sixties, and evidently enjoying his new career. He started the Plant Investment Company (called PICO), in April of 1882 as a legal entity so that his friends could buy in and join him in even more ventures. Henry Haines once described the arrangement very honestly, saying, "When it is decided to do a certain thing, build a piece of railroad for instance, they figure out what each is to pay and they send in their checks for the amount."

Members of PICO were carefully chosen, and included Morris K. Jesup, a New York banker and the owner of a railroad supply house; William T. Walters, a Baltimore merchant who was also buying bankrupt railroads; and Benjamin Franklin Newcomer, a Baltimore banker. Invited also were General Henry S. Sanford, then a senior officer of Adams Express and a landowner in Florida, and Henry M. Flagler, one of the wealthiest members, who was still busy accumulating millions thanks to Standard Oil.

Henry Plant next turned his attention to the Gulf of Mexico. He wanted to link his railroad lines from Charleston all the way through to steamships heading towards the rich ports of New Orleans, Mobile, and Pensacola, and also Key West and Cuba. The Live Oak & Rowland's Bluff Railroad was built as a first step toward that goal, although Rowland's Bluff (later re-named Branford after Plant's hometown), only had access to the Gulf via the Suwannee River.

Once the connection was made, Plant needed a steamboat on the Suwannee. He would settle for nothing less than a well-run system, so Plant bought his own line of steamboats. He must have smiled as he thought back to how he had mopped decks on a steamboat five decades earlier! Wisely buying several steamboats that already had successful routes on other Florida rivers, he re-named them the "People's Line." In January of 1883, a People's Line steamboat was transferred to Branford, which meant that Plant had service from Charleston to the Gulf of Mexico.

There was no stopping him now! Plant had bought and built railroads and he owned a steamboat line. He had already made transportation more convenient for anyone traveling into Florida, but there was much more to do. He still wanted his own port on the Gulf of Mexico, directly accessible by railroad track.

Chapter 4

Young Henry Flagler

Henry Morrison Flagler was born in Hopewell, New York, on January 2, 1830, into a poor but caring family. He completed the eighth grade at school and as soon as he was given permission to do so, Henry traveled to Ohio, by foot and by boat, to work at a store owned by his half brother's relatives. Fourteen-year-old Flagler received a warm greeting from the family when he arrived, and particularly from his good friend and half brother, Daniel M. Harkness. The two boys worked together in sales at L. G. Harkness & Company, Dan's uncle's store in Republic, Ohio.

At first Flagler's salary was five dollars a month, plus room and board, for working six days a week. However, it was soon obvious that he was ready for more responsibility. Raises in pay followed, and Flagler was pleased because he was determined never to be poor again. His enthusiasm and thrift impressed his relatives and everyone he met, earning him respect and trust at an early age. He was on his way to creating his own life.

At age twenty-three, Flagler married Dan's uncle's daughter,

Mary Harkness, and together the devoted couple had three children. Henry Flagler became a partner in Harkness & Company, but also tried other businesses. He made money and he lost money, learning always from both successes and failures. In the mid-1800s there were many entrepreneurs sniffing out a way to make a fast fortune, and Flagler's opportunity came when he met John D. Rockefeller.

Once the Civil War was over, America was on a path to becoming an industrial nation, and there was a huge need for oil. In 1867 Flagler joined Rockefeller and Samuel Andrews in an oil refining business, which just a few years later was incorporated as the Standard Oil Company. Rockefeller, the president of Standard Oil, and Flagler, both the secretary and treasurer, lived near each other on Euclid Avenue in Cleveland, Ohio, and frequently walked to work together, talking business along the way. Their business continued to grow, and the offices were eventually moved to New York City.

Even without formal schooling in legal matters or construction, Flagler was placed in charge of drawing up contracts and overseeing the building of new refineries. His partners learned that they could count on Flagler's ability to think clearly and concisely after considering all the options, and they knew that every detail would be

⊛ John Davison Rockefeller was a disciplined person even as a young man. The story is told that he once took so much time thinking about each and every move in a game of checkers that his opponent became frustrated. When asked to hurry, Rockefeller absolutely refused, replying that he was playing to win, not to lose.

Henry Morrison Flagler at forty years of age. 1870.
(Courtesy of the State Archives of Florida)

completed to the best of his ability. He created precise, clear contracts and insisted on nothing but the finest construction for their refineries. Since the oil was shipped by some of the many railroads then being built rapidly in the North, Flagler also met many railroad owners, learning a lot about that up-and-coming mode of transportation.

Since Standard Oil was growing larger and richer every day, Henry Flagler spent long hours at his office. But in the evenings, he spent quiet hours reading to his wife, Mary, who was never in good health. Their happy times were interrupted, however, when Mary became very sick. Her doctor recommended that she spend the coldest part of the winter in the South.

In 1878, Flagler and Mary traveled to Jacksonville. Mary's health improved in just a short time, and Henry Flagler tried to relax, noticing the warmth, the lovely flowering trees, and the beauty of the picturesque and meandering St. Johns River. He also noticed very clearly the need for better hotels and activities in Florida. His high-pressure job up North was on his mind, though, and after a few weeks, with Mary feeling much better, Flagler felt the need to return to his office. Mary could have stayed very comfortably, but she chose not to remain in Florida without her husband.

With Standard Oil growing so rapidly, Flagler encouraged Mary to go alone to Florida during the following winters, but she would not leave her family. On May 18, 1881, Flagler's beloved Mary died.

Flagler, by this time very wealthy, was devastated by his loss. Realizing that no amount of money could buy his wife's life back, the affairs of Standard Oil Company suddenly became much less important. He had reached his goal of never having to worry about being poor again, but he had lost what was most dear to him. To clear his mind totally, Flagler concentrated his thoughts on something entirely different.

He rented a luxurious estate in Mamaroneck, just north of New York City, called "Satan's Toe" because the grounds reached out into the waters of Long Island Sound. His half-sister, Carrie, took care of his children there, and Flagler spent time with them that summer, trying to get over the depression of losing his wife. Henry Flagler, after years of extremely hard work and pressure, realized the need for a change in his life.

The following year he bought Satan's Toe, re-naming it "Lawn

Beach." Stepping down from most of his responsibilities at Standard Oil, Flagler put his effort into renovating the forty-room house and grounds. His friends were amazed at the hidden talents of this business tycoon with experience only in building oil refineries. Flagler even designed a new chandelier, made of brass and crystal, which weighed more than a thousand pounds! Many friends came to visit and were totally amazed at the transformation. Flagler was happy, knowing he had taken on a new challenge and succeeded.

The distraction worked so well that fifty-two-year-old Henry Flagler, still grieving yet healthy and filled with life, knew he needed another project. He had a million-dollar fortune, had retired from Standard Oil, and had an enormous amount of creativity and ambition. He needed a productive way to spend his time and money.

Ida Alice Shourds, who had helped to care for Mary Flagler in her illness, became the second Mrs. Henry Flagler on June 5, 1883, in New York. That winter, the couple took a honeymoon trip to Florida. This time, however, they were not going for their health. Flagler was curious to see how the state had changed since his visit with his first wife, and he wanted to know why his New York friend, Henry Plant, was so interested in Florida. Flagler was already a member of the Plant Investment Company, which was investing in Southern railroads and heading even farther south. Flagler needed to see Florida again for himself.

Flagler and Ida Alice traveled south to Jacksonville by railroad, an uncomfortable trip with many delays and changes. Despite this, Flagler immediately noticed the growth and vibrancy in the city. They stayed for a few days at the new St. James Hotel. Quite elegantly built of brick and wood, this was a far cry from the older hotels that simply provided rooms, mostly for invalids. Already known as a comfortable

A drawing of the Tocoi depot on the St. Johns River as it looked in 1877.
(Courtesy of the State Archives of Florida)

resort, the St. James had not only electric lights, but even bowling
alleys and billiard rooms! Since Flagler was also anxious to see St.
Augustine, the Flaglers took a leisurely ride on a steamboat along
the scenic St. Johns River to Tocoi, and then took the bumpy little St.
Johns Railway into St. Augustine.

The old city was delightful, even though there were no large
hotels. It was a particularly cold winter in the North that year, but
in St. Augustine there were warm breezes blowing through the
many flowering trees. The abundant fresh fruits and vegetables were
delightful. Flagler immediately realized what his friend Henry Plant
had seen in Florida. There were so many possibilities in the state.
People could come for their health, but also to enjoy or even farm
in this bountiful land. Florida was just on the cusp of enormous
growth. Flagler's alert, creative eyes were wide open to Florida's huge
potential.

His zest for life was returning, and Henry Flagler imagined a larger picture for St. Augustine. He had renovated Lawn Beach in New York and his friends had flocked to see his newly redecorated home. Surely he could do something for this city that had not seen much change in years. It needed a hotel, and not just *any* hotel, but a *resort* hotel, one larger and grander than anything seen yet. Flagler had certainly heard the story of Ponce de León searching for a Fountain of Youth in the area. Perhaps this self-made tycoon thought he might find his own Fountain of Youth in St. Augustine.

Flagler and Ida Alice left for New York but made plans to return to St. Augustine the very next winter. He knew now why Henry Plant was investing in Florida, and he was thinking about a possible new career for himself in Florida too.

Chapter 5

Plant Railroads into Southwest Florida

While Henry Flagler was returning to New York with Florida
ideas running through his head, Henry Plant was busy with his
third entrance into Florida. Now the owner of both railroads and
steamboats, Plant wanted yet another link from Georgia into Florida.
At Climax, near Bainbridge, a railroad was built south to River
Junction (later Chattahoochee) in Florida, another perfect connection
for his steamboats. The Chattahoochee and Flint rivers meet at River
Junction to form the Apalachicola River, which runs to the Gulf
of Mexico. Cotton and produce from Georgia and Florida's rich
farmlands were transported to many markets via Plant steamboats and
railroads from this western port.

Plant was still not content, however, without his own port on
the Gulf of Mexico. The potential for such a port was enormous, and
there were several good options along Florida's west coast: Cedar Key,
Tampa Bay, and Charlotte Harbor. Cedar Key was an obvious first
choice, since David Levy Yulee's railroad connected that port with
the Atlantic coast. Plant tried to make an appointment to speak with
Yulee, but received no answer.

⚙ Cedar Key was a busy port known for its large stands of cedar trees. The cedar was much in demand for pencils, railroad ties, and more.

Looking further into the purchase of the Florida Railroad, Plant was told that even if he bought the railroad, he would not have access to the water's edge for terminal facilities. The Yulee family owned land in Cedar Key and did not want to sell much of it. They knew that land prices would skyrocket once Plant connected Cedar Key with the north.

Usually very much the gentleman, Plant grew angry. It is said that he responded: "I will wipe Cedar Key, Florida, off the map! Owls will hoot in your attics and pigs will wallow in your deserted streets!" He would find his own way farther south— to Tampa.

Plant decided to build his own railroad, naming it, ambitiously, the Live Oak, Tampa & Charlotte Harbor Railroad. It would be built through thick Florida woods. Work on the railroad was begun southeast from Rowland's Bluff (Branford) towards Fort White and High Springs. At Newnansville in Alachua County, however, Plant's workmen unexpectedly came across workmen from another railroad on almost the same route. The Florida Southern had a charter to build north to Lake City, close to Live Oak, and had already built tracks from Palatka to Gainesville. Plant was very interested to learn that their charter also stated that they could build to "the waters of Tampa Bay and Charlotte Harbor." Whoops!

Since Florida was in need of railroads, duplication of efforts seemed pointless, so Plant talked with the owners of the Florida Southern. Finding that they were having financial difficulties, he made them an offer, with a few contingencies. *If* Plant could link his railroad to theirs where the two lines met, and *if* the Florida Southern would agree to allow him to be the one to build to Tampa, Plant would agree to become a partner with a controlling interest in their line. He would also help them build farther south, along their own route, to Charlotte Harbor.

The owners of Florida Southern agreed, and Plant had turned a challenge into an opportunity. He also realized he had better get to Tampa quickly, before any competition, possibly even the Florida Transit (Yulee's cross-state Florida Railroad), reached that port. He modernized the Florida Southern's track as far as Gainesville, built a link from Fort White on his line to reach Lake City, and included other little settlements along the route. The people of Brooksville and Micanopy were slightly off the path, but they contributed money to be used for an extension to their towns so that they, too, would be linked to the north by rail. A bonus from this deal was his new acquaintance with Franklin Q. Brown, the Florida Southern's young president, who became one of Plant's close friends and associates.

Again Plant was on his way to Tampa. Again another opportunity appeared in his path.

A line starting from Sanford *also* had a charter to reach Tampa. The South Florida Railroad had run out of money after completing track from Sanford to Kissimmee via Orlando. The story is told that Plant's friend, Henry Sanford, and James E. Ingraham were walking together in Jacksonville one day when Sanford noticed Plant on the other side of the street. Sanford pointed to the elderly gentleman wearing a long black broadcloth coat and silk hat, and said: "That is a man I think you ought to know. I rode with him on my last trip down from New York."

Ingraham, an official of the South Florida Railroad, was delighted to meet Plant and invited him on a ride he was planning to

Kissimmee. Plant agreed, and on the day of their trip, Ingraham was at the Sanford dock when Mr. and Mrs. Plant, Henry Haines, and others arrived on the elegant steamboat *Henry B. Plant*. They then rode with Ingraham on his new railroad to Kissimmee. As the train chugged through freshly cut Florida forests, it is said the passengers were attended to by staff members wearing blue uniforms and white gloves. Ingraham had made his good impression, and after Plant talked to his advisors, the two men agreed to terms.

By May of 1883, Plant's company PICO owned a controlling interest in the South Florida Railroad. Plant's friend Henry Sanford was happy to know that the town named for him would thrive, and again Plant got a bonus in the transaction. James Ingraham became a trusted, close friend and wise advisor, and later, the friend and employee of another Henry—Henry Flagler.

Plant again thought he had his way to Tampa, then received yet another offer, one that would benefit him even more. The state government knew that Tampa was an excellent location for a port/railroad connection, so it had given several charters for track to be built to there. The Jacksonville, Tampa & Key West Railway (a *very* ambitious name!) also had a charter, which allowed the company to build from the St. Johns River to the Gulf of Mexico at Tampa. And because of the importance of this rail connection, the state promised one thousand *more* acres per mile of track than the South Florida was to receive. Plant realized that company too was short on money. PICO again had the advantage, but there was one catch.

In June of 1883, as Plant read the fine print on the charter of the JT&KW, the owners made sure he noticed the expiration date. Seventy-four miles of track had to be built through thick wilderness by January 24, 1884, just seven months away. Many thought it

⚙ Towns sprouted like weeds along the route of the railroad. Haines City and Plant City were two of them. Both were named in honor of the people who brought the much-wanted railroad to the area.

impossible, but Plant and his advisers were sure it could be done. Plant and his investment company bought the charter and, finally, started building to Tampa.

Later, when Henry Plant was asked why he chose that area for his railroad, he answered that

> when I first drove across the country from Sanford
> . . . I found Tampa slumbering as it had been for
> years . . . It seemed to me that all South Florida
> needed for a successful future was a little spirit and
> energy, which could be fostered by transportation
> facilities. . . I made a careful survey of the situation,
> calculated upon its prospects and concluded to take
> advantage of the opportunity.

Surveyors and engineers were sent out to mark the route so that workers could begin at both ends, working furiously through a hot, humid Florida summer. Henry Haines supervised the whole job, and entrepreneurs watched the route of the track so they could buy land. They knew that the price of even deep woods would go up dramatically when the track was finished.

The workmen labored night and day, and finished just before the deadline. Plant, Haines, and Ingraham rode a ceremonial train into

Tampa in the company of a jubilant Governor Bloxham. The state's economy could now grow, and Plant at last had his port on the Gulf of Mexico, linked by railroad through to northern cities!

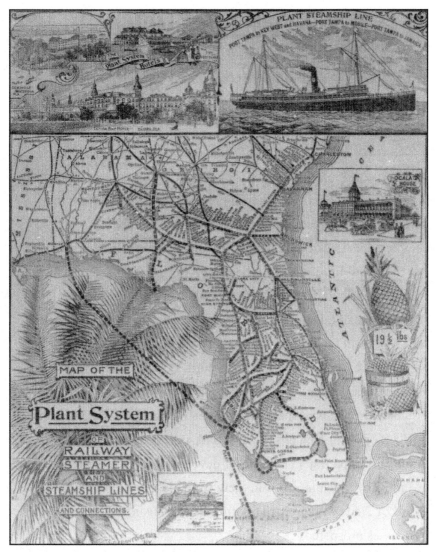

This map of the Plant System shows all of the railroad track and steamship lines that Henry Plant owned. (Courtesy of the State Archives of Florida)

Chapter 6

The Plant System

By February of 1884, the people of Tampa could set their watches by
the whistle of the trains as they approached or departed from their
new depot. By September of 1886, the South Florida Railroad had
completed its track between Sanford and Jacksonville, closing that
gap in the rail line, and all of the track had been changed to standard
gauge. The trip north was then not only more comfortable, but had the
added bonus of taking less time and not requiring changes along the
way. The Plant Steamship Company could also continue the trip for
passengers or packages going on to ports along the Gulf of Mexico
and the Caribbean, including Cuba and Jamaica.

Fort Brooke was finally deactivated by the U. S. War Department
in 1883, opening up that sixteen-square-mile property right on
beautiful Tampa Bay to be sold for development. People were coming
to Tampa by the trainload, and there were plenty of jobs. Tampa's
Board of Trade worked hard to bring in new businesses, and those
businesses prospered.

With Plant steamships now available to bring shipments of
tobacco back from Cuba, Vicente Martinez Ybor and others made

the decision to relocate their thriving cigar businesses from Key West to Tampa. Ybor, aware that the town was growing quickly, invested in its growth by purchasing seventy acres just outside of town. He built affordable housing for the streams of factory workers immigrating to the neighborhood. Ybor City grew, and Plant built a rail line to connect it with the factories, which were in town. Tampa was designated an official port of entry into the United States and, by 1887, had its own U.S. Customs House. Rutted, sandy streets were paved, sewers were installed, and the people even enjoyed evenings out at the Opera House.

Boom times stopped abruptly in 1887, when the words "yellow fever" were heard throughout the city. Highly contagious and often fatal, yellow fever had occurred in Florida before, but that hot, steamy summer brought one of the worst outbreaks yet known. There was no cure at the time, and the only thing the terrified people could do was to leave the city as quickly as they possibly could. They knew there was something in the sweltering summer air in the city that caused the yellow fever, and they refused to return until the weather was cooler. With their workers fleeing, Ybor and many other businessmen wondered if moving to Tampa had been a mistake.

Henry Plant was in New York when the epidemic first hit, but was in constant touch with everything going on in Tampa and found

⊛ A Tampa physician named Dr. John P. Wall, whose wife died of yellow fever in 1871, suggested that mosquitoes carried yellow fever. People didn't believe him, however. Later, a team of Army doctors headed by Dr. Walter Reed proved that Wall was right.

out quickly. He immediately boarded his private railroad car and hurried South. Plant knew he had to help the town that had grown so much because of his railroad. He needed to reassure the people, and businesses, that Tampa was still a safe place to live.

Although Plant may have originally thought that he would just connect the railroad to the port and allow the townspeople to build up the town themselves, this situation called for a bold step. Plant made two announcements that showed without a doubt his own faith in the growing settlement. He said he would change the port so that larger vessels could dock closer to shore and create a large, world-class facility for ships arriving in Tampa. He also promised to build a large, world-class hotel.

Many Tampa businessmen heard Plant's resolve and also stood firm. Within six months, Tampa was growing again.

Engineering studies showed that just nine miles beyond the city,

The Inn at Port Tampa and wharf. (Courtesy of the State Archives of Florida)

there was plenty of room for a large port with deeper water close to shore. Opening on February 5, 1888, Port Tampa was indeed world-class.

A wharf almost a mile long was built out into Tampa Bay. It could accommodate not only twenty-six ships at one time, but also railroad cars that could be loaded or unloaded by huge cranes that were several stories high. Warehouses built out on the wharf could hold freight for the next steamship or train, and the Inn at Port Tampa was built to house passengers awaiting a boat ride to the Caribbean or the next train into Tampa. The Inn was built directly on the busy wharf, and right over the water!

Steamships of the Plant Steamship Line were easily recognizable leaving the wharf, with a cross and a "P" for Plant on the smokestack. Plant ordered two new ships, which he named the *Mascotte* and the *Olivette*. The ships were as elegant as their names. Plant steamships did a lively business from Port Tampa to Key West, Havana, Nassau, and Jamaica. Later they could even be seen in the north Atlantic, taking passengers and freight to Canada's maritime provinces of Nova Scotia and Prince Edward Island.

Thanks to such excellent facilities, Tampa continued its growth. Phosphate, needed to make fertilizers, was shipped by the carload

⚜ The Inn at Port Tampa, which opened in 1890, advertised: "The waters teem with fish, and it is a literal truth that you may catch one or more out of your chamber window while dressing, ring for a bell boy, and fifteen minutes later have it served hot and inviting for your breakfast."

The sleek Plant steamship *Mascotte*. (Collection of Seth H. Bramson)

out of Port Tampa, as well as so many cigars that Tampa was called the "Cigar Capital of the World." Even with different names for the railroads under the Plant System, his customers could always count on excellent quality service, and constant expansion.

Other communities, also in need of railroad service, were added to the Plant System routes. Georgia service expanded farther west with Plant's acquisition of the Brunswick & Western in the 1880s, which he included as part of his Savannah, Florida & Western. In Florida the small towns of Leesburg, Longwood, Apopka, and others were reached by branch rail lines. Railway facilities at Sanford were updated, and a new, more modern passenger depot was built for the town.

Making good on his word to the Florida Southern to help them build their track to the Charlotte Harbor area, Plant made sure construction to the south continued while he was busy in Tampa. Track reached Trabue (later Punta Gorda) by July of 1886. The three-story Hotel Punta Gorda was built and became a favorite with sportsmen.

Henry Plant and PICO had close to a monopoly on rail service in central and western Florida, and Plant was ready to build a grand hotel.

Chapter 7

Two Henrys and Two Hotels

While Henry Plant was busy on Florida's west coast, Henry Flagler, eleven years younger than Plant, planned another trip to Florida. As a member of the Plant Investment Company for several years, he certainly was aware of what Plant was creating with his railroad system, and Flagler had recently become enchanted with the historic town of St. Augustine. With enough money to do whatever he wished, Henry Flagler was ready for a new adventure.

On February 17, 1885, Henry and Ida Alice Flagler left frigid New York temperatures behind for a train ride all the way through to Jacksonville, Florida. Railroad lines were better connected along the east coast, partly because of Henry Plant, and they arrived at their warmer destination just two days later, in their own private railroad car. After again staying at the St. James Hotel in Jacksonville for a week, they left their private car to cross the St. Johns River by ferry. On February 25, they rode a new line, the Jacksonville, St. Augustine & Halifax River Railway, from south Jacksonville to the gates of the old city.

Henry Flagler's private car had a luxurious sitting area, dining area, bedroom, bathroom, and kitchen. It is now located in Flagler Kenan Pavilion at Whitehall in Palm Beach. (© Flagler Museum Archives)

Jacksonville and St. Augustine had for years been a destination for invalids, and both Plant and Flagler had sought the warmth there for their ill wives. But on this trip Flagler watched Northerners in excellent health filling a new, luxurious hotel called the San Marco in St. Augustine, where Flagler and Ida Alice were also staying. The old town was bursting with new life, with freshly painted, newly constructed cottages standing out among the houses from the past. The new residence called Villa Zorayda really stood out—it was built

of cement and coquina shell in a Moorish, or Middle Eastern, design.
The city streets were still deep sandy paths, but at least there was
more to see and do.

The idea of a new hotel stayed in Flagler's mind. Friends said
later that Flagler had always wanted to own a hotel, but he wanted
not just any hotel, but a *resort* hotel. He wanted one that would entice
wealthy visitors to stay not just for a few days, but for the whole
winter season. While Flagler was in town, the businessmen of St.
Augustine put on a delightful celebration of the landing of Ponce de
León in 1513, and soon after this Henry Flagler made his decision. He
would build his own resort hotel and name it the Hotel Ponce de Leon.

Flagler bought land for the hotel before heading back to New
York with his wife on April 1, 1885. He would return within two
months with an architect and a business adviser.

Henry Flagler was fifty-five years old, and certainly not ready for
retirement. Asked later about why he built the Hotel Ponce de Leon,
Flagler answered, "For about fourteen or fifteen years, I have devoted
my time exclusively to business, and now I am pleasing myself."
Flagler, as Plant already had, was launching a whole new career—in
Florida.

Flagler chose a young architect from New York, Thomas
Hastings, and his partner, John M. Carrère, to design a hotel that
would reflect St. Augustine's rich Spanish heritage. James McGuire
and Joseph McDonald, who had recently completed the San Marco
Hotel, were chosen to build the structure using local coquina shell
and concrete. The luxurious interior was accented by Louis Comfort
Tiffany, who later became world famous for his exquisite stained glass
designs. Henry Flagler would have nothing but the best.

It was only when Flagler's workers had problems getting some

Henry Flagler's elegant Hotel Ponce de Leon. Undated. (Courtesy of the State Archives of Florida)

of the building materials needed for the hotel that he turned his sights to railroads. Hoping the Jacksonville, St. Augustine & Halifax River Railway company would modernize its line not only for his supplies but later for his guests, Flagler talked with the owners. When they would not upgrade the line, Flagler bought the railway on December 31, 1885. He then went on to create a railroad that served his purposes by immediately doubling the weight of the rails, changing to standard gauge track, buying new equipment, and building a drawbridge across the St. Johns River at Jacksonville. At the time, Flagler might have thought this was the only railroad he would ever own. He was just

⊕ Carrère and Hastings also designed the U. S. House and Senate office buildings in Washington, D. C., the New York Public Library, and many other public and private buildings.

⚙ Flagler once said about the building of the Hotel Ponce de
Leon: "I think it more likely I am spending an unnecessary
amount of money in the foundation walls, but I comfort
myself with the reflection that a hundred years hence it will
be all the same to me, and the building better, because of my
extravagance." The walls were built four feet thick, and the
building is still in use today as Flagler College.

interested in the construction of his hotel.

The Hotel Ponce de Leon opened its doors on January 10,
1888, for a private celebration and dinner for the architects, builders,
artists, railroad officials, and many others involved with the planning
of the hotel. Awesome in its appearance, the magnificent Spanish
Renaissance–style Hotel Ponce de Leon rose up four stories high,
with 240 guest rooms, and spread out over most of a five-acre lot. The
opening to the public was two days later, and newspapers called the
hotel one of the grandest in the world.

Flagler's hotel brought thousands of people to St. Augustine,
and he continued to build up the city, funding churches, schools,
and a hospital. He grieved when his daughter, Jennie Louise Flagler
Benedict, died of childbirth complications in 1889. He built Memorial
Presbyterian Church in remembrance of his beloved child.

Knowing that his hotel would draw many more Northerners,
Flagler had Carrère and Hastings design a less formal hotel, the
Alcazar, across the street. He then bought a third hotel, the Casa
Monica, which he re-named the Hotel Cordova. The town's year-round
population doubled in less than one year.

Flagler had reason to smile. His hotels were successful, and he had enjoyed the creativity of the projects. He had built a more vibrant city, using his money not just for himself, but to give employment and better lives to others. He had spent more than two million dollars, but the work and the money had been worth it. He had left grief and stressful work behind him. Perhaps, in helping others, he had found his own Fountain of Youth.

❀

Henry Plant had been invited to the grand opening of the Hotel Ponce de Leon and was interested in its huge success. This was probably about the time that Plant first thought about having some fun with his friend. Plant already owned hotels in Florida. He had stayed at the Seminole Hotel in Winter Park, a large inn along his railroad track, and was so impressed with the service and elegance of the place that he bought it. There was also his Port Tampa Inn, which stayed busy at the wharf on the Gulf of Mexico. But he had promised the people of Tampa a very elegant hotel, and now he would go all out.

The Tampa Bay Hotel was Henry Plant's personal project at first, and he wanted only to please himself and Mrs. Plant with its design. Later, however, the Plant Investment Company took it on as one of its hotels. One of Plant's goals for the hotel was that it be totally different from Flagler's.

The Tampa Bay Hotel was designed to reflect not the historic Spanish heritage of Florida, but a very popular trend of the time: Moorish, or Middle Eastern, architecture. Houses were built in Moorish design even in old St. Augustine, and having a Middle Eastern room in one's home was the rage. There was a fairy-tale feeling in the Moorish influence, and Plant decided to bring that look to the wilderness of Florida.

John A. Wood, an architect from New York, was asked to design this Islamic Revival–style fantasy, and Plant knew the location of his grand hotel was very important. The businessmen in town wanted the grand hotel near their stores, but Plant decided it should be off by itself, surrounded only by ancient oak trees with Spanish moss hanging on the branches. The ideal spot was across the Hillsborough River, so Plant bought land there. He also asked the city to build a bridge over the river for passengers and had his own workmen build a railroad bridge. On July 26, 1888, the cornerstone was laid amid much excitement and anticipation.

The older settlers in Tampa had barely gotten used to the idea of huge locomotives puffing into their town when suddenly there appeared a truly marvelous sight across the river. The completed Tampa Bay Hotel rose five stories into the air (Flagler's hotel was four stories high), had 511 rooms (Flagler's had 240), and spread out over a

Henry Plant's fantastic Tampa Bay Hotel, with a view of the Lafayette Street Bridge and the Hillsborough River. (Courtesy of the State Archives of Florida)

quarter of a mile. The building was not made of wood like most of the Tampa houses, but of brick and cement to make it fireproof.

The fantastic Tampa Bay Hotel was lighted by electricity at night, and by day reflected the Florida sunshine, particularly on its roof, with thirteen silver minarets topped by crescent moons The whole scene seemed to be right out of *Arabian Nights*. The awesome structure was called "one of the modern wonders of the world" and a "palace in the wilderness." The interior was just as grand, since Plant and Margaret had brought back more than forty carloads of fabulous furnishings from a trip to Europe.

Thousands of invitations were sent out for a formal Grand Opening held in February of 1891. One, of course, was sent to Henry Flagler, and he may have attended.

That evening, more than two thousand guests arrived. Spotlights on the minarets and Chinese lanterns twinkling in the gardens illuminated the gala affair. At 9:30, a short burst of music stopped all conversation. Mr. and Mrs. Henry Bradley Plant made their grand entrance, with Margaret wearing a Paris-designed gown. Guests danced to a special song written especially for the occasion, the "Tampa Bay Gallop." The evening was a success, and Plant could relax, certain that the more than $3,000,000 cost of the hotel and furnishings had been worth every penny.

He had certainly out-done his friend Flagler!

Chapter 8

Flagler Railroads into East Florida

Whether they were focused on competition or new adventures, the two Henrys never relaxed for long. While Henry Plant was busy building in Tampa and enlarging his Plant System of railroads, Henry Flagler was setting his sights on other railroads with tracks into, and south of, St. Augustine.

Flagler already owned the Jacksonville, St. Augustine & Halifax River Railway, the only all-rail route into St. Augustine from the north. There were two other ways to reach the town, and both were via the St. Johns River. The St. Johns Railway came from Tocoi and the St. Augustine & Palatka Railway came from Palatka, both sharing one track for part of their trip into the old city. Realizing the great advantage of linking with the busy St. Johns River and its steamboats, Flagler bought one line, and later, the other. Flagler modernized the track and built a new terminal near his Hotel Ponce de Leon in St. Augustine. Three efficient rail routes brought visitors into town, and three large hotels awaited their arrival. And Flagler owned them all.

Word got around about this very rich man named Flagler. The

businessmen in nearby Palatka tried to interest Flagler in buying land in their town as well, but at first he was not interested. The story is told that later, when the entrepreneur wanted to buy some land there for his railroad, they refused to sell to him.

Their refusal did not bother such a creative man. Flagler kept his eye on the future and bought another railroad. With this choice, Flagler started on his way down the east coast of Florida.

The narrow-gauge logging road called the St. Johns & Halifax River Railway was a natural extension of Flagler's St. Augustine & Palatka Railway. The fifty-mile short line had been built for hauling logs out of the thick woods between Palatka, on the St. Johns River, and Daytona, on the Halifax River and the Atlantic Ocean. Flagler realized the advantage of bringing a modern railroad a bit farther south. It would be enormously helpful for the farmers in little settlements along the route as well as the loggers. He bought the SJ&HR, modernized it, and by 1890 had started a real estate boom in all the towns along the route, particularly at Daytona. Flagler's railroad line now lived up to its name: the Jacksonville, St. Augustine & Halifax River Railway. He also bought another hotel.

A large hotel had been built between the clear water of the Halifax River and the sandy beaches of the Atlantic Ocean just north of Daytona, but the owners of the Ormond Hotel had financial problems. A more efficient railroad and the Flagler touch for the Ormond were both badly needed. Flagler became the new owner and re-named it the Ormond Beach Hotel, adding even more rooms. Recognizing the management skills of the previous owners, Flagler asked them to stay on. He also built a trestle bridge across the Halifax River so track could reach it directly from his main line. And thus Flagler did it again—the hotel was soon another successful link in

Jacksonville, St. Augustine & Halifax River train. Daytona Beach area. 1880s.
(Courtesy of the State Archives of Florida)

what was becoming the Flagler chain of hotels.

Henry Plant and Henry Flagler were both finding that once they opened one door, another seemed to open right behind it. Plant wanted a better transportation system for Florida, and as a result of his work toward this goal, he opened up part of the state to the southwest. Flagler's quest to own "a hotel" led him to open up the east coast. By 1890, Flagler also owned 110 miles of track, a true railroad system. It is very likely, however, that Flagler did not intend to go farther at that time. Beyond Daytona there were no other railroads to buy. It was wilderness to the south, so Flagler stayed in one place for a while.

He continued to modernize what he already owned, and he also saw the need for a better bridge across the St. Johns River at

Jacksonville. Flagler talked with his engineers, who honestly told
him they were not sure it was possible to build such a wide bridge
over water that was ninety feet deep. His engineers were constantly
pushed to the limit of their abilities. The story is told that he asked,
very simply, if they could build piers in such deep water. After the
engineers talked together for a moment, they decided that they could.
Flagler replied: "Then build it."

The Jacksonville Bridge Company was incorporated, and
construction of an all-steel bridge was begun. When completed in
January of 1890, it was one of the finest bridges in the Southern
states, and Flagler's guests could travel comfortably from New York to
his hotels and all the way to Daytona.

The late 1800s were an exciting time in America. Trains could
travel for long distances, and entrepreneurs with their eyes wide
open were making fortunes. George M. Pullman realized the need
for a sleeping car for overnight train trips, so he founded the Pullman
Palace Car Company in 1867. Pullman cars were a sensation, and by
January 9, 1888, the day before the grand opening of the Hotel Ponce
de Leon, the first through train, with Pullman cars, left New Jersey
for Jacksonville. It made the run in 29 hours and 50 minutes. Crowds
actually gathered along the way to marvel at the train that was making
history. Later dubbed the "Florida Special," that train became the

⊛ A booklet printed by the South Florida Railroad in 1887
described a passenger riding in a Pullman car in this way:
"Soft cushioned divans receive his body; a delicate luncheon
is served at any hour; an airy 'smoker' invites him to gossip
with his fellow guests—they cannot be travelers. No, he is the
guest of a hotel on wings."

pioneer luxury train to sunny Florida.

While Flagler's train terminal remained in Daytona, his interests took him other places as well. He bought land for a farm in Hastings, a small town along his railroad track. He paid farmers to raise potatoes, and he learned more about the possibilities of Florida agriculture. At another stop on the line, San Mateo, he established citrus groves. The people living in that town openly showed their gratitude for Flagler and his railroad, and many good friendships were formed. To show his appreciation for their warm welcome, Flagler one day invited San Mateo's several hundred residents to visit St. Augustine, where he treated them to dinner at the Hotel Alcazar. Flagler put up with some jealousy and misunderstanding as he accomplished more in Florida, but in those towns he was a hero.

Daytona grew to a city of almost one thousand residents. Another Flagler hotel might have been built there, but like Palatka, the businessmen were not encouraging. So Flagler bought boats.

South of Daytona the Halifax River is called the Indian River, and Indian River citrus was known for its distinct and excellent taste. Citrus and pineapple growers there previously had to take their produce all the way to Jacksonville to reach Northern markets. Thanks to the closer railroad terminus Flagler built, however, boats loaded with bumper crops (crops from a particularly good harvest) could now dock at Daytona. Knowing that it would be helpful to those farmers, Flagler bought some boats for use along the Indian River.

But boats and oranges and potatoes did not keep Henry Flagler busy for long. As people wondered if he would take his railroad farther south, Henry Flagler himself took a boat trip to consider some new options.

Amazed at the pristine beauty of what he had already seen of the east coast of Florida, Flagler went as far as Palm Beach and was impressed anew. Coming upon a beautiful land covered with hundreds of red royal poinciana trees, Flagler also saw the clear, clean waters of Lake Worth and the Atlantic Ocean. The delightful scenes all inspired Flagler to open up more of this gorgeous coast. He figured that his wealthy friends who could afford to go to the elegant Riviera resorts along the Mediterranean Sea in Europe could be lured into visiting his "American Riviera" instead. Before his trip was over, Flagler found out that the few residents there were definitely in favor of another of his resort hotels.

Chapter 9

The Flagler System

The Flagler railroad system soon faced totally new challenges. Flagler had built and bought hotels in towns that were already starting to grow. He had also bought existing railroad lines, where someone else's workmen had hacked through almost impenetrable woods, and modernized them. But he had never been a pioneer—he had never had his own workmen build track through woods and swamps where wild animals had lived undisturbed for years. Neither had he gone into a community of a dozen or so homes and turned it into a major resort area. That was about to change, though. From this time on, Flagler, with his eyes wide open, expanded his—and Florida's—horizons.

He needed advice. Two very important people, among many others, agreed to join the Flagler team. James Ingraham, earlier the president of the South Florida Railroad and advisor to Henry Plant, was asked to work with Flagler railroads and land companies. Joseph R. Parrott, a graduate of Yale University Law School and attorney for Henry Plant, became Flagler's legal advisor and later president of the whole company.

Taking the next step, Flagler in 1892 was granted a charter from

❋ Ingraham had recently taken some men on an expedition through the Everglades for Henry Plant, who wanted to know if railroad track could be built from Fort Myers on the west coast to Miami. After a dangerous trip across the Everglades, Ingraham advised Plant and also Flagler that the best way to reach Miami was via the east coast. That was interesting news to Flagler.

the State of Florida to build brand new railroad track to the south, not only to Palm Beach, but all the way to Miami. For every mile of new track laid, Flagler's railroad was given eight thousand acres of land. Realizing he had also outgrown the name of his company, the Jacksonville, St. Augustine & Halifax River Railway became the Jacksonville, St. Augustine & Indian River Railway in 1892. At the time, however, he probably didn't intend to use the charter through to Miami. He was anxious to reach Lake Worth, next to Palm Beach.

On June 17, 1892, Henry Flagler was ready, so his project supervisor gave the word to about 1,500 workmen to start the tremendous job of clearing the way until they reached Rockledge. Along the way they came across little settlements, where people looked on in amazement and cheered the coming of the railroad. After a rough, sweaty summer's work, the Jacksonville, St. Augustine & Indian River track reached New Smyrna in November of 1892 and Rockledge by February of the following year.

At Rockledge, officials evaluated the work on the railroad that had already been done. They found that while the work had been difficult, it had been completed successfully, so Flagler again gave the go-ahead to the workmen. They would build through to Palm Beach.

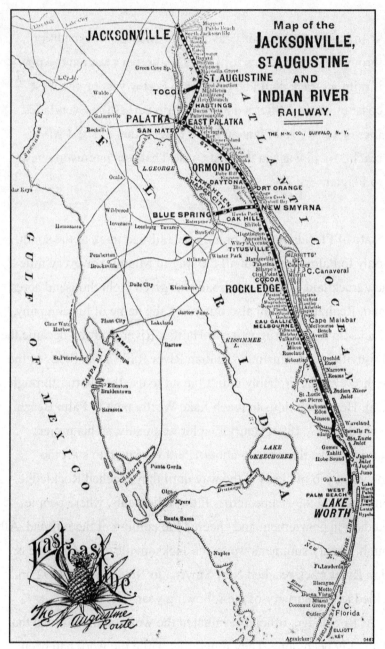

Map of Jacksonville, St. Augustine & Indian River Railway from Jacksonville to Lake Worth. (Courtesy of the State Archives of Florida)

Along with Ingraham and Parrott, Flagler made a second trip to Palm Beach to buy land, as well as to listen to the handful of families there cheer because they would finally have easy transportation to the rest of Florida and the North.

It is known that the Plants and the Flaglers also spent time together, at Rockledge and on a cruise to the Bahamas aboard one of Plant's steamships. The friendly competitors probably shared stories about how they were "pleasing themselves" in Florida.

Flagler's railroad reached Fort Pierce by the following January, while smaller branch lines sprouted out east and west to connect small communities with the main track. One existing short-line train could have made Flagler's work a little easier. The Jupiter & Lake Worth Railroad was already taking passengers and freight along eleven miles of the route. Flagler offered to buy the small line, but his offer was refused. He bypassed their route, and by 1895 the "Celestial Railroad" had withered away.

For his Hotel Royal Poinciana in Palm Beach, Flagler again chose McGuire & McDonald, the firm that had built his very successful Hotel Ponce de Leon in St. Augustine. Overlooking Lake Worth, the wooden Hotel Royal Poinciana stood tall at six stories high (Henry Plant's Tampa Bay Hotel was only five stories!), with 540 bedrooms (Plant had 511). What had been an overgrown area with only dirt paths between the few houses soon became a whole new world.

◉ The Jupiter & Lake Worth Railroad was called the "Celestial Railroad" because the towns along its route were Jupiter, Juno, Mars, and Venus.

Streets were paved and electricity was available before the grand opening in February of 1894.

It was a little farther to travel for Northerners, but with through, modern railroad service to the South, the Hotel Royal Poinciana was another success for Flagler. Guests gladly came to what was called "the Queen of Winter Resorts." Riding in comfort all the way to the train depot at West Palm Beach, a side track over a wooden bridge took guests, still in their private cars, right up to the front door of the hotel. Special track was built for parking of the private cars, and at times during the winter season, those tracks were very crowded. The wealthy owners stayed in suites at the hotel, while their servants stayed in the private cars.

Flagler relaxed, and many thought again that he was ready to stay in the area. Thinking some guests might prefer to stay closer to the ocean, he built a second hotel in Palm Beach in 1895 and called it the Palm Beach Inn (later renamed The Breakers). The original structure burned to the ground a few years later, but Flagler gave the word for it to be re-built and it still stands today. Once again he rested, but then was abruptly reminded that he had been asked to go farther south.

Chapter 10

Florida East Coast to Miami

For about ten years, both Henrys had advertised the virtues of
Florida's warm climate for tourism, farming, and business. Both had
helped to change the image of Florida. No longer was it a place of
invalids and wilderness. Instead, thanks to the influence of Flagler
and Plant, Florida was becoming known as a vibrant, sophisticated,
healthy, and always warm place to visit and live. Both were then
stunned when their promise of constant warmth in Florida was
shattered.

The winter of 1894–1895 was one of the coldest winters in
Florida history.

Several nights of freezing temperatures destroyed the citrus crop
and then the citrus trees down to their roots. This happened not only in
north Florida, but as far south as the middle of Dade County. Many of
the rare tropical plants on the grounds of the Tampa Bay Hotel froze,
and in Palm Beach, even large coconut palms were ruined. It was
devastating for the state's farmers. With their annual harvest gone and
the fear that it could happen again, farmers talked of leaving.

An orange grove during the 1895 freeze. (Courtesy of the State Archives of Florida)

Flagler immediately sent James Ingraham to see what could be done for the farmers, including the offer of loans so their families could survive through the winter. Seeds were distributed so that perhaps other crops might be planted. Ingraham was also asked to report back to Flagler on the extent of the freeze, and to see if any part of Florida had not been hit. He headed south, finding devastation for miles until he approached Miami, where the abundant citrus trees were alive and well.

Miami had become a small community around Fort Dallas, which had been the Army post back in the Seminole War days. Several families lived where the lovely Miami River emptied into Biscayne Bay, a pretty isolated place then. With no road through the thick woods to reach the settlement, mail was delivered by a barefoot mailman walking down the coast! William Brickell and his family were some of the settlers living in the area. They had made a living there trading with the Indians.

Julia Tuttle owned land at the old Fort Dallas, and she wanted to see the area grow. When Flagler had started building his railroad down the east coast, Tuttle asked him several times to continue his track down to the Miami area, but he had not been interested. The sudden freeze changed his mind.

On his return from the trip south, Ingraham reported that the freeze had not reached the Miami area. He had even brought back fresh citrus blossoms for Flagler to see. Ingraham also gave a glowing account of the Biscayne Bay area and described the royal palm trees and many varieties of flowers along the coastline of the Atlantic Ocean. Impressed by the report, just a few days later Flagler made that same trip, together with Parrott and his builders, McGuire & McDonald.

Flagler and his aides talked with Julia Tuttle, who further enticed the railroad builder by offering him land she owned for a hotel and railroad terminal. The Brickell family, and others, promised more. State land was, of course, also forthcoming as Flagler opened up more of Florida's east coast for development. Flagler thought about the farmers whose crops had been destroyed by the freeze, and he realized they could have jobs building the railroad or his new hotel. Flagler talked over all the possibilities with his advisors. Then, on June 12, 1895, he agreed to extend his railroad the sixty or so more miles to Miami. Surveys of the road were begun. He already had the charter!

The name of Flagler's line again needed to be changed. "Florida East Coast Railway," or FEC, was a much more accurate name for a railroad that extended from Jacksonville to Miami. The FEC was

incorporated in September of 1895, and all of the Flagler railroads
came under the one name. Flagler, still enjoying himself, was very
aware of his influence on the state. It is said that he once told his
friends: "My domain begins at Jacksonville." Floridians themselves
joked that the abbreviation for Florida, "Fla," really stood for
"Flagler!"

The way through to Miami was a huge job for the workmen, and
of course Flagler wanted the job done as quickly as possible. Flagler
wanted to get the track finished by the first day of February and
wanted to have the brand new hotel ready by the next winter season.
They didn't meet that schedule because of major obstacles between
West Palm Beach and Miami. Reaching farther south in Florida meant
hotter, steamier weather in very thick woods. Huge vines, undisturbed
for years, were tough to break through, and alligators and mosquitoes
were ferocious in their battle to keep the intruders out. The
manchineel trees had to be avoided because they were very poisonous.
Ironwood trees were dense enough to break one axe after another and
could only be removed by dynamite.

But workers, whose chopping and sawing and detonating of
dynamite could be heard for miles, finished more than sixty miles
of track in an amazingly short time. Loud cheers greeted the first
passenger train arriving on the shores of Biscayne Bay in April of
1896, setting off not only a large celebration, but a land boom.

Julia Tuttle was right. She had been certain that her town would
grow with the coming of the railroad. Within three months, the
population of Miami soared and land prices went sky-high. Tents were
set up on any available land to house the many new settlers. Land was
sold to developers, and cottages sold easily at $1,500 each. Flagler's
publicity people further helped the boom by calling the east coast of

Florida the "American Riviera" and declaring that "The East Coast of Florida is Paradise Regained." Flagler reserved one section of town for homes for his workmen. By July 28, 1896, there were already enough residents for Miami to be officially incorporated as a city.

There were jobs for all who came. As he had done for other cities, Flagler had streets paved, electricity brought in, sewage and water lines installed, and public schools established. Land was donated for churches and municipal buildings. One challenge was finding a good base for roads. Limestone rock, available locally, was found to work well, but it is said that it was so bright in the sunshine it gave people headaches!

The little town called Miami had changed a lot by the time Flagler's Hotel Royal Palm opened to the public in early 1897. The huge, 680-foot-long building was five stories high, with an observation platform around the top floor that had an awe-inspiring view of the river, the bay, and the Everglades. Painted what was called "Flagler yellow," the hotel had electric lights, as well as a golf course, billiard room, ballroom, swimming pool, and even a separate dining room for maids minding the children. Superb service and constant amusement kept visitors coming back. The Hotel Royal Palm became the center for Miami social life.

⊛ Of course friend Henry Plant was invited to the grand opening, and the story is told that he could not resist reminding Flagler that he too had built a "palace in the wilderness." Plant inquired: "Friend Flagler, where is this place called 'Miami'?" Flagler smiled, and wired back: "Friend Plant, just follow the crowds!"

Flagler dredged a channel into the Miami River and deepened Biscayne Bay for larger ships. Harry Tuttle, Julia's son, ran a passenger boat from Miami to Key West. Boat docks were kept busy unloading passengers or freight from Jacksonville, Tampa, Pensacola, and the Bahamas. Flagler created the Florida East Coast Steamship Company and bought a steamship, the S.S. *Miami*. Miami became the fifth largest city in Florida less than fifteen years later and has been called "the city that Flagler built."

Flagler did make money from the sale of land and from his hotels, but it was some time before he realized any profit from the trains, because of the cost of fuel. The locomotives mostly burned wood of the pine tree called fat pine, and Flagler preferred that they buy it from individual lumbermen along the train route. The engineer picked up his wood and gave the lumberman a "wood ticket," which the lumberman then turned in to the railroad office for payment. However, the supply of fat pine dwindled over the years, and by 1920 locomotives were running on coal-burning engines.

Although Flagler had much to keep his mind occupied, it was a hard time for him personally. For several years it had been clear to him that his second wife, Ida Alice, was suffering from mental illness. In 1899, even with the care of the best doctors available, she was declared hopelessly insane. Afterward, Flagler was deeply depressed, but knew he must get on with his life.

 Henry Flagler's second wife, Ida Alice, was under the care of the best psychiatrists available during her illness. After the divorce, she received excellent care in a private institution, where she remained for the rest of her life.

Moving his permanent address to Palm Beach, Flagler was able to obtain a divorce in 1901. His third marriage was to Mary Lily Kenan, a woman he had known for several years. Mary Lily requested a "marble palace" as a wedding gift. Since cost was not an issue, Flagler had Carrère & Hastings design a grand new residence for them close to his hotels. "Whitehall," with its 55 rooms, cost $2.5 million to build and $1.5 million to furnish. The *New York Herald* described their incredible home as "more wonderful than any palace in Europe!"

Mary Lily and Henry Flagler's "marble palace," Whitehall. 1902. (© Flagler Museum Archives)

Chapter 11

Remember the Maine!

Along with the huge challenges during the two Henrys' years in
Florida, there was also applause. The area surrounding old Fort Dallas
had been called "Miami" for some time, but was not official until the
city's incorporation in 1896. To show their gratitude to Henry Flagler
for the change in their lives, some of the area's residents, including
many of Flagler's loyal employees, wanted "Miami" to be changed to
"Flagler." When Henry Flagler heard of the idea, he suggested instead
that they keep "Miami," the city's old Indian name, which was also the
name of the river and was said to mean "sweet water."

Henry Plant had his day of glory when the Cotton States and
International Exposition—held in Atlanta, Georgia—set aside October
28, 1895, as "Plant System Day." Thousands of his friends and
employees attended to show their appreciation for Henry Plant and
his extraordinary service to America's Southern states. A silver loving
cup was presented to Plant, which, he was told, was filled with the
best wishes of his employees and friends. Plant looked over the sea of
faces, recognizing many friends he had made over the years. He spoke

> ⚙ "I regard work as one [of] the essential principles of my
> success—my personal supervision of every detail of my
> business. I believe in never leaving to others what I can do
> myself." —Henry Bradley Plant

to the crowd, expressing his grateful thanks for the wonderful tribute,
and before the meeting ended, 76-year-old Henry Plant shook hands
with each one in attendance. Later Plant called that day the happiest
of his life.

And while Flagler was building railroad track to Miami, Henry
Plant was still working at extending his own railroad track and even
building another hotel. He had seen beautiful Clearwater Beach, just
north of Tampa on the Gulf of Mexico, and decided to build not only a
hotel, but a community there. His Hotel Belleview at Belleair opened
the same year—1897— as Flagler's Hotel Royal Palm opened in
Miami. Plant extended a branch railroad line there and his hotel soon
became a meeting place for millionaires.

Their commitments to Florida were still not finished. Both
Henrys worked with other railroad owners on the design and building
of a large train terminal and train yards in Jacksonville. Completed in
1897, the Jacksonville Terminal was another improvement for trains
entering Florida. With its beautifully landscaped grounds, it became
an impressive entrance to the now-thriving city of Jacksonville.

Another war was brewing, however, that created problems for all
railroad owners in Florida, but particularly for Henry Plant.

For about two years, workers in Tampa factories had quietly
rolled Cuban tobacco into cigars while a reader informed them of
the latest news from Cuban newspapers. By 1897 the factory readers

were reading aloud reports of Cubans fighting for their country's
independence from Spain. Since many Cuban-Americans had
relatives in their native country, they began encouraging the rebels by
sending money for the cause. When Spanish Army General Valeriano
Weyler learned about this, he immediately placed an embargo on
Cuban tobacco into America. If the Cuban-Americans helped the
revolutionaries, he would ruin their business.

Weyler did not count on Henry Plant. Before his plan could
be put into effect, the *Mascotte* and the *Olivette* sped to Cuba with
orders from Plant to fill every nook and cranny on both ships with
tobacco and to then very quietly return home. The tobacco was stored
in Tampa warehouses, and business went on. Weyler's embargo had
failed.

The fighting continued, and there was soon danger of all-out
war. Franklin Q. Brown, in charge of hotels for the Plant Investment
Company, visited Cuba and brought back news to Plant and also to
President William McKinley in Washington, D.C. With war possible,
Brown probably reminded the president that Tampa could be a
convenient port from which to send troops.

The U. S. battleship *Maine* blew up and sank in Havana harbor
on the night of February 15, 1898. Plant's *Mascotte* and *Olivette*
were again immediately dispatched, this time to bring back survivors
and any Cubans wanting to leave the country. Those wanting Cuban
independence shouted "Remember the *Maine*!" over and over, and
two months later, war was declared.

The Spanish-American War transformed Tampa for a while.
Plant railroads brought thousands of American soldiers and carloads
of supplies into town. Although the Tampa Bay Hotel had already
closed for the season, it re-opened so that military personnel could

be housed in its gracious rooms. The *Mascotte* and the *Olivette* were used as hospital ships. Famous and not-yet-famous people were seen in the busy Tampa streets. These included Clara Barton, founder of the American Red Cross, and Stephen Crane, author of *The Red Badge of Courage*, who would write another story while staying at the Tampa Bay Hotel. "Teddy" Roosevelt, who three years later became the twenty-sixth president of the United States, drilled with his own company of "Rough Riders" in Tampa before leaving to fight in Cuba.

The 10th U.S. Cavalry embarking for Cuba at Tampa. 1898. (Courtesy of the State Archives of Florida)

The Spanish-American War, also called the War for Cuban Independence, was short, but brought Florida a lot of publicity and Plant a lot of revenue. Many soldiers went to Tampa, but Henry Plant and Henry Flagler both kept a careful eye on their hotels, railroads, and steamships as they tried to keep order. As soon as the soldiers left, the hotels were made ready for the next season and overworked railroad tracks and ports were repaired. Only after making sure all was well could both men relax again. Henry Plant was almost 80 years old, and although he looked forward to a new century, he was tired.

By June of 1899, Henry Plant, still president of Southern Express Company, had done a lot in Florida and the Southern states. He owned hotels in many parts of the west coast of Florida, from Punta Gorda to Clearwater to Kissimmee. He had bought or built railroads in Georgia and connected them with railroads in Florida. He had lived a full life.

On June 22, 1899, an exhausted Plant went into his New York office to work, but by that evening, he felt very weak. The next afternoon, Henry Bradley Plant died at home. He was buried in Branford, Connecticut, and his long-time friend Henry Flagler was at the funeral.

When the news reached Tampa, there was a huge sense of loss. All Plant System hotels and trains were draped in black for a period of mourning. Newspaper headlines around the world told of how Tampa and the whole South had grown because of this man. The Plant System in 1899 had more than 2,200 miles of railroad stretching from Charleston, South Carolina, to Montgomery, Alabama, though the majority of his track was in central and western Florida. Henry Bradley Plant had become one of the wealthiest men in the South, particularly in terms of respect from his friends.

Henry Bradley Plant. Undated. (Courtesy of the State Archives of Florida)

Chapter 12

"Flagler, You Need a Guardian!"

Henry Flagler was seventy years old on January 2, 1900, but there was still another adventure ahead for him, perhaps his greatest. He said:

> I was born with a live oak constitution, and it is only within a year or two that I have known of the possession of any organs. My diet has always been simple and the only excess I believe I have indulged in has been that of hard work. I have, however, one ailment (old age) which is incurable, and that I am submitting to as gracefully as possible. I am quite sure, however, that I possess as much vitality and can do as much work as the average man of forty-five.

Flagler, saddened by the loss of his friend Plant, was nevertheless ready to proceed with his own work on the east coast of Florida.

The question, it seemed, was: would Flagler attempt the building of a railroad across the Keys to reach Key West? He had already

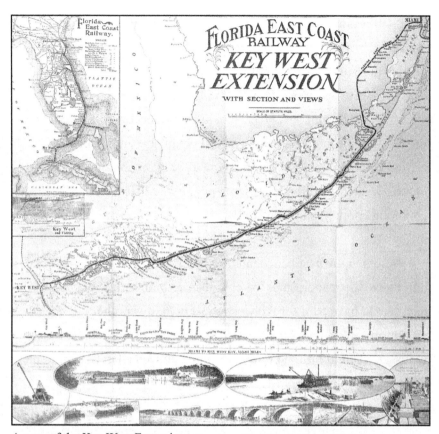

A map of the Key West Extension. (Courtesy of the State Archives of Florida)

⊛ Jefferson Browne in 1894 said: "The hopes of the people of Key West are centered in Henry M. Flagler, whose financial genius and public spirit have opened up three hundred miles of the beautiful east coast of the state. The building of a railroad to Key West would be a fitting consummation of Mr. Flagler's remarkable career."

spent $30 million in the state, and St. Augustine, Ormond Beach, Palm Beach, and Miami were thriving cities. And yet, there was that creative urge to do even more!

Key West was more than 100 miles beyond the end of the Florida peninsula. Its federal naval base had been modernized, and a channel for ships had been deepened during the Spanish-American War. The city had a large population, with about 17,000 inhabitants. Key West's citizens wanted a railroad and some people predicted that if Flagler lived long enough, he would be the one to build that railroad through to Key West.

Others in the past had wanted to take on this enormous job, but didn't have the resources or the engineering knowledge. Flagler, even then, would have paid for the work to be done by another builder, but not one could be found. So many educated people said it was impossible. Build railroad track over and between islands right in the path of major hurricanes? Absolutely crazy!

Flagler took his time and looked at all the options. If a canal were built at Panama, Americans would want a deepwater port nearby for security for the canal and also for shipping. Flagler thought Cape Sable, at the very tip of Florida's mainland, could perhaps be that port. He sent William Krome through the Everglades to survey that area, and to find out if the depth of the water there was suitable. It is said that William Krome, happy just to be alive when he returned from the expedition through the watery area, reported back to Flagler: "There isn't enough fill on the face of the earth to build a railroad across the Everglades."

In 1903, the Hay-Bunau-Varilla Treaty made clear that the United States would indeed build a canal at Panama, and Flagler made his decision. The Florida Legislature approved the construction

of the FEC's Key West Extension. By summer of 1904, the Florida
East Coast Railway pushed to the very end of the Florida mainland,
along Cutler Ridge to Homestead. Beyond this there was no more
continuous dry land.

Some of Flagler's friends were sure he had lost his mind. When
George M. Ward—minister at the chapel Flagler built in Palm
Beach—heard of Flagler's decision to connect the mainland to
Key West by rail, his reply, very simply, was: "Flagler, you need a
guardian."

One last time, in 1905, Flagler checked with the man who had
become vice president and general manager of the Florida East Coast
Railway, Joseph R. Parrott. The story is told that Flagler looked
Parrott straight in the eye and said, "Joe, are you *sure* this railroad
can be built?" Parrott, who had spent hour after hour reading endless
reports and surveys and had carefully evaluated every aspect of the
project for years, looked back at his boss and said very certainly, "Yes,
I am sure." Those were the exact words Flagler wanted to hear.

The Florida East Coast Railway would go to sea. Flagler, Parrott,
and other executives toured the proposed route, and Flagler took the
opportunity to announce to the delighted crowds in Key West that the
railroad was finally coming.

The optimism that Flagler felt was being felt all over America
at the time. President Theodore Roosevelt was in the White House,
where he was saving land for national parks and exuding health and
enthusiasm for the future. The Wright brothers had just demonstrated
that man could fly, and Henry Ford and others were perfecting an
even more convenient new mode of transportation: the automobile.
Huge numbers of immigrants were coming to America, seeking new
opportunities. Americans could do whatever they set their minds to do!

Henry Flagler, however, did not just run on enthusiasm. This was his biggest project yet, and he was very aware of the dangers ahead. This was not an engineering firm building the extension. It was a railroad company. Anyone he hired to head up the project had to be ready to stretch his limits again and again. Not only was there bridge design and surf levels and water depths to deal with, but also the proper care and feeding of thousands of workmen several places at once throughout the Keys!

Yet Flagler knew he could relax—he had found the best man possible to be the project manager.

Chapter 13

Florida East Coast to the Horizon

Joseph C. Meredith had a reputation for taking on jobs that others considered impossible. He had just completed construction of a huge pier made of reinforced concrete for the Mexican government. Since reinforced concrete was thought to be the best material available for the columns on the railroad bridges between the Florida Keys, Flagler asked Meredith to come see him. The interview was short. Meredith said the job could be done and that he could do it. Flagler asked when he could start. Meredith said he could start immediately. Meredith packed and headed for Key West!

William J. Krome, one of the original surveyors, became principal assistant engineer of the project. Meredith and Krome, extremely competent builders and leaders, took on the job knowing very well that they had just accepted one of the most challenging and monumental jobs in America at that time. Their names would definitely be in history books, whether it be in glory or shame. It was an immense project, but what a wonderful opportunity for anyone who enjoyed a challenge!

With everything in place, newspapers in many parts of the world called the project "Flagler's Folly" and predicted monumental failure. Asked how he could build railroad track over more than 100 miles of water and islands, Flagler is said to have quipped: "It is perfectly simple. All you have to do is to build one concrete arch, and then another, and pretty soon you will find yourself in Key West."

When ground was broken at Key West for a railroad terminal, a wild celebration followed. The dreams of the people of Key West were finally coming true. Crews of workmen were sent to several stations along the Florida Keys, designated by mile markers similar to, but not the same as, the ones used in the Keys today. From there, the work began.

There were surprises along the way. On the first leg of the project, the conventional digging machines got stuck in the thick Everglades muck and sawgrass, so floating steam dredges with their large buckets had to be brought in instead. On reaching Key Largo, the workmen found a lake right in their path that had not been on the original surveys. "Lake Surprise" put their work fifteen months behind schedule, but the engineers took it in stride as just the latest challenge. Plans were made, and plans were changed. This had never been done before. Every day was a new challenge.

The work crew consisted of men from many different countries. Working together was sometimes difficult, especially under the harsh conditions. They were given transportation to the work site, but some just looked at the mosquitoes and the other men sweltering in the intense heat and left immediately. It was lonely work. Many of the Keys were deserted little islands that years before had hidden pirates preying on Spanish ships loaded with treasure sailing through the Straits of Florida.

The workmen who did stay on were well cared for. There were as many as 4,000 workmen on the job at one time, and camps set up along the Keys allowed the workers to sleep in clean beds, eat nutritious meals, and have access to fresh, clean water. So much concern had been put into this matter that, amazingly, there was not one epidemic of illness during the whole seven years of the project.

The weather, however, could not be controlled.

In order to make up time lost at Lake Surprise, everyone worked through the 1906 hurricane season. The project's leaders later regretted that decision, but learned a lot from what happened as a result.

Weather forecasting in the early 1900s was primitive. Barometers to indicate air pressure had been invented, though Flagler's foremen mostly used a homemade model, a sprig of seaweed in a tall glass container. In September and October, the height of the hurricane season, foremen checked the glasses regularly.

On the evening of October 17, 1906, the seaweed rose steadily as the outside air pressure dropped ominously. Those who could took cover, but that hurricane caused the greatest loss of life on the whole extension project. Camps exposed to the winds were destroyed, and some men were washed out to sea by huge surging tides. Reportedly, more than one hundred men died, and some track and even large pieces of machinery were totally wrecked.

Though distraught by the loss of life, Flagler and Meredith knew that the work on the Key West Extension must go on. It is told that Meredith, after being shaken by the news, wrote in his diary: "No man who cannot stand grief should be connected with this project." Changes were made in the work camps for greater safety, new equipment and supplies were ordered, and work on the Key West

Extension went on.

At Long Key in January of 1908, the first of three great viaducts for the railroad was completed. One hundred and eighty concrete arches majestically spanned over the two and a half miles of water between Long Key and Conch Key. This span was tremendously difficult to build and specialists were needed in some areas of the work. Divers from Greece, usd to diving deep for sponges in their native country, were hired to work on the deep foundations. When the viaduct was finished, Flagler was so thrilled with its magnificent look that he changed the official seal of his railway. From that time on, the seal showed a train on the Florida East Coast Key West Extension rolling over the arches of the awesome Long Key viaduct. Flagler even built a fishing camp at this Key, which became a great hit with sportsmen over the years.

Construction on the Key West Extension. (Courtesy of the State Archives of Florida)

Four years later, Flagler's railway hugged Florida's east coast for 477 miles, stretching from Jacksonville to about halfway through the Keys. Flagler was getting older, and showing signs of age. Beyond Knights Key, there was another huge expanse of water to be bridged to the next key in the chain. This distance was so great that standing on one end of the span, the other end was beyond the horizon, due to the curvature of the Earth. A port at Knights Key could have been used for steamship access to Key West instead of extending railroad track there. After much research and consideration the decision was made to take the railroad to Key West as planned. The engineers tackled this latest challenge with fervor. From Knights Key, the span now called the Seven Mile Bridge was built in four separate sections as it attached itself to the next key in the chain.

It was during that construction, however, that Flagler received terrible news. Joseph C. Meredith, his amazing chief construction engineer and trusted friend, had died while on the job. The news devastated him.

Flagler's feelings were poured into a funeral service for Meredith, a fitting ceremony for a person he held in such high esteem. Flagler also placed a stone with a bronze plaque at his gravesite in a Miami cemetery. The loss of Joseph Meredith was deeply felt by his many co-workers, but Meredith's work would go on.

Chapter 14

"My Dream Is Fulfilled."

William J. Krome, at thirty-two years of age, was asked to take over for Meredith as engineer-in-chief. He immediately said yes. Krome, who had been second in command of the project, knew exactly how to proceed. C. S. Coe, division engineer, became Krome's assistant, and together they mapped out their schedule. Their goal was to complete the extension through to Key West by 1910. But they hadn't reckoned on another massive hurricane.

On October 10, 1909, a huge storm crossed Cuba, headed straight for the Keys. Winds of up to 125 mph hit Marathon, but foremen had plenty of warning this time, thanks to the telegraph lines that had been strung from Miami. The Seven Mile Bridge withstood the storm with few repairs needed along the track, but about thirteen lives were lost. One year later, another hurricane hit the Keys, but that time not a single employee was killed.

Hurricanes and other delays took precious time from the completion of the project. Flagler, still interested in every detail of the work, was showing the strain of the huge undertaking, particularly

❀ Cameras were available during the time of the building of the building of the Key West Extension. Several workers took photographs and wrote in journals, so we have on-the-spot records of happenings at that time.

after Meredith's death. So he began to allow others, especially Joseph Parrott, to make more decisions. The men worked round the clock as Flagler's health grew more fragile. The question was no longer: "Can we get to Key West?" The workmen now asked themselves instead: "Can we make it to Key West in time?" There was a good possibility that the only thing keeping Flagler alive was the anticipation of fulfilling his dream. They set another deadline, this time for January 2, 1912—Flagler's eighty-second birthday.

Workmen watching Henry Flagler's train on its way to Key West. 1912. (Collection of Seth H. Bramson)

The big event was nearly twenty days late, but a collective sigh of relief (none so great as Krome's!) was heard when the Key West Extension was completed while Henry Flagler was still alive. The project had taken seven years and nine months. On January 21, 1912, workers put the last span in place in the Knights Key trestle, and the "impossible" line of railroad track linked Key West to the mainland of Florida.

A very grateful Henry Flagler spent that night in Miami so that he would be fresh and rested for the next day, such a highlight in his already full life. On January 22, 1912, the first official train arrived at Key West at 10:43 A.M., filled with officials of the Florida East Coast Railway as well as invited dignitaries and friends. The weather was beautiful, and in the last car of the "Extension Special" was a tired, but ecstatic, Henry Flagler.

An enormous crowd of about 10,000 people had gathered at the Key West terminal, including representatives from Europe, Mexico, and Central and South America, along with the assistant secretary of war, Robert Shaw Oliver, sent by President William Howard Taft.

A huge cheer went up when eighty-two-year-old Flagler stepped out onto the platform of his private car. The city was three days into the "Over the Sea Railroad Celebration," which was to end that night with a banquet honoring Flagler for completing the monument task. Bands played, a chorus of a thousand children sang patriotic songs,

⊛ W. R. Hawkins worked for Flagler's railroad. He wrote in his journal on January 22, 1912: "Passenger train to Key West. Uncle Henry's train ran through to Key West this morning. . . . Uncle Henry's train was the first passenger train to cross the bridge."

and diplomats gave speeches. The mayor of Key West welcomed
Flagler. George W. Allen, president of the Chamber of Commerce,
presented him with a gift from the people of Key West. Another
special gift was presented by the men who had labored on the
project for seven long years. Everyone in attendance knew that the
"impossible" project had only been completed because of Flagler's
total and unswerving devotion to the task.

Henry Flagler was overcome with emotion. He told the thousands
before him, "I thank God that from the summit I can look back over
the 25 or 26 years since I became interested in Florida with intense
satisfaction at the results which have followed." As he was escorted to
the reviewing platform, however, he said, "I cannot see the children,
but I can hear them singing."

At eighty-two years of age, Henry Flagler was nearly blind,
but his mind remained clear and alert, and his happiness knew
no bounds. As he left the platform, he placed his hand on Joseph
Parrott's shoulder and whispered: "Now I can die happy. My dream is
fulfilled."

Flagler lived another year after his triumphant train ride into
Key West, but his body was very weak. He fell descending a stairway
at Whitehall, and at ten in the morning on May 20, 1913, Henry
Morrison Flagler died peacefully in his own bed.

A memorial service was held three days later in St. Augustine,
the city he and his first wife had visited the first time just thirty-
five years before. His pallbearers included Joseph Parrott, James
Ingraham, and others who had become close friends with the
enthusiastic man. He was buried at the church he himself had built,
Memorial Presbyterian Church in St. Augustine, near his first wife
Mary and his daughter, Jennie Louise, and her baby.

Henry Morrison Flagler. 1912. (Courtesy of the State Archives of Florida)

Flagler, a legend in his own time, left a personal estate in 1913 of as much as $100 million. He had spent millions developing Florida and left behind monuments that will keep his name alive in the exciting history of the state. He had built or bought railroad track along the entire Atlantic coast of Florida between Jacksonville and Key West. Another extension to Okeechobee that ran from New Smyrna on his main line all the way through to the farms and settlements in the south-central part of the state was completed in 1915.

Early in the twentieth century, two major construction projects were completed. One was the Panama Canal. Another was the Key West Extension. It is interesting to consider that the Panama Canal was built by a country, and the Key West Extension was built by Henry Flagler and his Florida East Coast Railway. The Key West Extension, once called "Flagler's Folly," was later called the "Eighth Wonder of the World."

Afterword

Americans built railroads, and railroads built America. The two Henrys, described by a mutual acquaintance, John Sewell, as "best of friends," were accomplished businessmen before they ever set foot in Florida. Once they were there, both obviously enjoyed themselves as they promoted Florida as an almost ideal place to vacation and live.

Plant and Flagler tremendously increased the economic development of the state, unlocking the beauty of Florida for all to come and enjoy. They each respected the other's territory, wasting little time on rivalry. With a lot of hard work and imagination—and despite some almost unbearable sorrow—Florida's frontier land became an American Riviera.

In 1902 the Plant System railroads, with 2,235 miles of track, became a part of the Atlantic Coast Line Railway. Southern Express became part of American Railway Express, which was later re-named Railway Express Agency. Henry Flagler's railroads, with 765 miles of track, kept the name Florida East Coast Railway, and it's the name the railroad is still known by today.

While Plant used both his own and other people's money, including Flagler's, Flagler spent a huge portion of his fortune in Florida. It is thought that he never asked J. R. Parrott if he would make a profit on any project. Flagler simply said, "Build it." He did say, very often: "If it wasn't for Florida, I'd be quite a rich man today." Both men, however, still had large fortunes when they died.

As a direct result of both Henrys' railroads and hotels, the stage was set for the Florida we know today. Changes in the twentieth century came fast. Henry Ford and others built cars and trucks. In

1914, the Panama Canal opened, World War I started, and people could travel by airplane. In 1936, the Key West Extension was converted to a two-lane roadway for cars, using many of the sturdy viaducts built by Henry Flagler's workmen. And now, in the twenty-first century, Plant's Tampa Bay Hotel is the heart of the University of Tampa, while Flagler's Hotel Ponce de Leon houses Flagler College.

Both Plant and Flagler prepared Florida for the future. Flagler's good friend, the Reverend George Ward, recalled that Flagler was interested not only in the present, but most of all, in the future. Entrepreneurs of any age catch that same spirit.

The two Henrys, friendly competitors who together opened up a state, will live on in the colorful history of Florida.

Selected Chronology
of Railroad History

1500s – Narrow-gauge wooden wagons and rails were in use in coal mines in central Europe.

1712 – Thomas Newcomen, an Englishman, invented the steam engine.

1804 – Richard Trevithick, a brilliant English engineer, completed the first steam-road carriage to carry passengers.

1807 – Robert Fulton modified a boat by adding paddle wheels and a steam engine, calling it the *Clermont,* and found it would travel against the current on New York's Hudson River.

1819 – Henry Bradley Plant was born in Branford, Connecticut.

1826 – One of the first railways in America was chartered in Massachusetts. It was three miles long, and had iron-faced rails. These "strap rails" became common in the United States.

1827 – A charter was granted to the Baltimore & Ohio Railroad Company.

1829 – The locomotive "Stourbridge Lion" was shipped to America. Horatio Allen took it on a successful run in Honesdale, Pennsylvania. Allen made the run alone because his friends were too frightened to go with him.

1830 – Henry Morrison Flagler was born in Hopewell, New York.

1830 – Peter Cooper, an American, completed his own American-built steam engine, the "Tom Thumb." Its first run was 13 miles— the railroad age had definitely begun.

1837 – In Florida, the Tallahassee–St. Marks line was in use.

1861–65 – During the Civil War, railroads were important for moving soldiers and supplies, but much track was destroyed.

1864 – George Pullman started making "hotel" cars.

1867 – The first patent for a refrigerated railroad car was granted.

1868 – Major Eli H. Janney patented the first effective automatic train-car coupler. Train cars would no longer have to be separated by hand, an extremely unsafe practice.

1869 (May 10) – The "gold spike" ceremony was held in Promontory, Utah, marking the completion of the Transcontinental Railway.

1869 – George Westinghouse, at only 22 years of age, patented the air brake, making trains safer.

1879 – Henry Plant bought his first railroad—the Atlantic & Gulf Railroad.

1882 – The Plant Investment Company (PICO) was started.

1884 – Plant's railroad—the Jacksonville, Tampa & Key West Railway—reached Tampa, Florida.

1885 – Henry Flagler bought his first railroad—the Jacksonville, St. Augustine & Halifax River Railway.

1895 – The name of Flagler's railroad system became the Florida East Coast Railway.

1899 – Henry Plant died.

1903 – The Ford Motor Company was incorporated, and the end of the train era drew closer.

1912 – The Florida East Coast Railway reached Key West.

1913 – Henry Flagler died.

1988 – The Tallahassee/St. Marks Historic Railroad Trail opened, running from Tallahassee to the coast. This walking/biking trail was built over the rail bed of Richard Keith Call's Tallahassee Railroad. "Rails to Trails" has converted unused train roadways to recreational trails in many parts of the state.

Glossary

charter – a document that grants certain rights or privileges

citrus – fruits such as lemons, limes, grapefruit, oranges, etc.

contingencies – dependent on something else (for example: an agreement made only as long as something else is agreed to)

controlling interest – when one person or group has more control over the running of a business than others in that same company

corporation – a group of people legally working together at a business

cusp – a point that marks the beginning of a change

entity – something in existence

entrepreneur – a businessman or one who has ideas for, or starts, a new business

freight – goods or cargo to be shipped

incentive – something that tempts a person to make a decision or to perform an action

incorporate – to include, to form into a corporation

innovative – considered to be something new

languish – to droop, to lose vigor or vitality

mode – a fashion, a way of doing something

Moorish architecture – style of architecture common in Spain during the Middle Ages, characterized by horseshoe arches and ornate decoration

oil refining – making oil purer

option – a choice

pristine – pure, clear, natural

recurrence – something that happens again

Riviera – a grand resort area in Europe along the Mediterranean Sea, including parts of France and Italy

steamboat – a shallow-draft boat, used on rivers and along coasts

steamship – an ocean-going vessel

terminus – the end of anything, or either end of a railroad line

venture – a risky undertaking

wither – to shrivel, decay

To See and Do

Many of the historical places mentioned in this book are open to the public. Here is a bit more information to help you decide where you'd like to visit.

Hotel Belleview at Belleair, Clearwater. Still used as a hotel (the Belleview Biltmore Resort), it is listed on the National Register of Historic Places. Called "The White Queen of the Gulf" since the wooden structure was painted white in the early 1900s, the hotel is currently closed for renovations, but will resume tours once it's reopened. Address: 1501 Indian Rocks Road, Bellair, Florida 33756. Website: www.belleviewbiltmore.com.

The Breakers, Palm Beach. Still used as a hotel, it is on the National Register of Historic Places. The hotel is open every day, but call ahead for historical tours given each Tuesday. Address: One South County Road, Palm Beach, Florida 33480. Website: www.thebreakers. com.

Hotel Ponce de Leon, St. Augustine. Now home to Flagler College, it is listed on the National Register of Historic Places. Historical tours are given here daily. Address: 74 King Street, St. Augustine, Florida 32084. Also of interest would be the Lightner Museum across the street (formerly the Hotel Alcazar). Website: www.lightnermuseum.org.

Tampa Bay Hotel, Tampa. Now functions as Henry Bradley Plant Hall at the University of Tampa and the Henry B. Plant Museum. It is listed as a designated National Historic Landmark.

Self-guided tours of the extensive museum are available. Address: 401 West Kennedy Boulevard, Tampa, Florida 33606. Website: www. plantmuseum.com.

Whitehall, Palm Beach. Listed on the National Register of Historic Places, Whitehall now houses the Flagler Museum. Self-guided, audio, or docent-led tours are available, as well as summer camps. See Flagler's private railcar on the grounds. Address: One Whitehall Way, Palm Beach, FL 33480. Website: www. flaglermuseum.org.

Selected Bibliography

Akin, Edward N. *Flagler: Rockefeller Partner and Florida Baron.* Kent, OH: The Kent State University Press, 1988.

Braden, Susan R. *The Architecture of Leisure: the Florida Resort Hotels of Henry Flagler and Henry Plant.* Gainesville, FL: University Press of Florida, 2002.

Bramson, Seth H. *Florida East Coast Railway* (Images of Rail/Images of America). Charleston, SC: Arcadia Publishing, 2006.

Bramson, Seth H. *Speedway to Sunshine: The Story of the Florida East Coast Railway.* Erin, Ontario, Canada: The Boston Mills Press, 2003.

Bramson, Seth H. "A Tale of Three Henrys," *The Journal of Decorative and Propaganda Arts, (Florida Theme Issue),* 1875–1945 no. 23 (1998): 112–43.

Brown, Canter. *Henry Bradley Plant: The Nineteenth Century "King of Florida."* Jean Katherine Stallings Educational Series. Tampa, FL: The Henry B. Plant Museum, 1999.

Gallagher, Dan. *Florida's Great Ocean Railway: Building the Key West Extension.* Sarasota, FL: Pineapple Press, 2003.

Graham, Thomas. *Flagler's St. Augustine Hotels: The Ponce de Leon, the Alcazar, and the Casa Monica.* Sarasota, FL: Pineapple Press, 2004.

Lenfestey, Hatty. *An Elegant Frontier: Florida's Plant System Hotels.* Jean Katherine Stallings Educational Series. Tampa, FL: The Henry B. Plant Museum, 1999.

Martin, Sidney Walter. *Florida's Flagler*. Athens, GA: The University
    of Georgia Press, 1949.

Mueller, Edward A., and Barbara A. Purdy, eds. *The Steamboat
    Era in Florida, Proceedings of a Conference*. March 24, 1984.
    Gainesville, FL: Florida Maritime Heritage Program, 1985.

Reynolds, Kelly. *Henry Plant: Pioneer Empire Builder*. Cocoa, FL:
    The Florida Historical Society Press, 2003.

Rinhart, Floyd, and Marion Rinhart. *Victorian Florida: America's Last
    Frontier*. Atlanta: Peachtree Publishers, Ltd., 1986.

Smyth, George Hutchinson. *The Life of Henry Bradley Plant: Founder
    and President of the Plant System of Railroads and Steamships
    and also of the Southern Express Company*. New York: G. P.
    Putnam's Sons, 1898.

Standiford, Les. *Last Train to Paradise: Henry Flagler and the
    Spectacular Rise and Fall of the Railroad that Crosses an Ocean*.
    New York: Crown Publishers, 2002.

Stewart, Laura, and Susanne Hupp. *Historic Homes of Florida*,
    Second Edition. Sarasota, FL: Pineapple Press, 2008.

Stowe, Harriet Beecher. *Palmetto Leaves*. Gainesville, FL: University
    of Florida Press, 1968.

Turner, Gregg M., and Seth H. Bramson. *The Plant System of
    Railroads, Steamships and Hotels: The South's First Great
    Industrial Enterprise*. Laurys Station, PA: Garrigues House
    Publishers, 2004.

Twain, Mark, and Charles Dudley Warner. *The Gilded Age*. New York:
    Oxford University Press, 1996.

References

Note: "Ibid." is short for the Latin word *ibidem*, which means "in the same place." Below, if you see "ibid.," that means a quote came from the same book as the quote before it did.

Chapter 1
Page 2. "We have taken the locomotives off the road...": Edward A. Mueller and Barbara A. Purdy, editors, *The Steamboat Era in Florida: Proceedings of a Conference* March 24, 1984 (Gainesville, FL: Florida Maritime Heritage Program, 1985), 67.

Chapter 2
Pages 5–6. "If you want to see a new and peculiar beauty...": Harriet Beecher Stowe, *Palmetto Leaves* (Gainesville, FL: University of Florida Press, 1968, facsimile reproduction of the 1873 edition), 112–13.

Chapter 3
Page 15. "There are two ways of getting to Jacksonville...": G. W. Nichols in *Harper's Magazine,* October 1870, as quoted in Seth Bramson's *Speedway to Sunshine* (Erin, Ontario, Canada: Boston Mills Press, 2003), 13.
Page 15. "When it is decided to do a certain thing...": Gregg M. Turner and Seth H. Bramson, *The Plant System of Railroads, Steamships and Hotels* (Laurys Station, PA: Garrigues House, 2004), 30.

Chapter 5
Page 25. "I will wipe Cedar Key...": Ibid., 19.
Page 25. "the waters of Tampa Bay...": Ibid., 34.
Page 26. "That is a man...": Kelly Reynolds, *Henry Plant: Pioneer Empire Builder* (Cocoa, FL: The Florida Historical Society Press, 2003), 145.
Page 28. "...when I first drove across the country from Sanford...": G. Hutchinson Smyth, *The Life of Henry Bradley Plant* (New York, G. P. Putnam's Sons, 1898), 77.

Chapter 6
Page 33. "The waters teem with fish...": Hatty Lenfestey, *An Elegant Frontier: Florida's Plant System Hotels,* Jean Katherine Stallings Educational Series (Tampa, Florida: The Henry B. Plant Museum, 1999), 11.
Page 34. "Cigar Capital of the World.": Tampa Bay & Company website, www.VisitTampaBay.com.

Chapter 7
Page 38. "For about fourteen or fifteen years...": Sidney Walter Martin, *Florida's Flagler* (Athens, GA: University of Georgia Press, 1949), 115.
Page 40. "I think it more likely I am spending...": Edward N. Akin. *Flagler: Rockefeller Partner and Florida Baron* (Kent, OH: The Kent State University Press, 1988), 121–22
Page 43. "one of the modern wonders of the world": Susan R. Braden, *The Architecture of Leisure: the Florida Resort Hotels of Henry Flagler and Henry Plant* (Gainesville, FL: University Press of Florida, 2002), 274.
Page 43. "palace in the wilderness": Canter Brown, *Henry Bradley Plant: the Nineteenth Century "King of Florida,"* Jean Katherine Stallings Educational Series (Tampa, Florida: The Henry B. Plant Museum,1999), 16.

Chapter 8
Page 47. "Soft cushioned divans receive his body...": Floyd Rinhart and Marion Rinhart, *Victorian Florida: America's Last Frontier* (Atlanta, GA: Peachtree Publishers, Ltd., 1986), 22.

Chapter 9
Page 54. "the Queen of Winter Resorts.": Edward N. Akin, *Flagler: Rockefeller Partner and Florida Baron*, 156.

Chapter 10
Page 58. "My domain begins at Jacksonville.": Quote from a letter dated February 15, 1898, to John Porter. Cited in Seth Bramson's *Speedway to Sunshine*, 52.
Page 59. "The East Coast of Florida is Paradise Regained.": Seth H. Bramson, *Speedway to Sunshine*, 53.
Page 59. "Friend Flagler, where is this place called 'Miami'?" Seth H. Bramson, "A Tale of Three Henrys," *The Journal of Decorative and Propaganda Arts* Florida Theme Issue, 1875-1945, no. 23: 117.
Page 60. "the city that Flagler built.": Sidney Walter Martin, *Florida's Flagler*, 150.
Page 61. "...more wonderful than any palace in Europe!" Laura Stewart and Susanne Hupp, *Historic Homes of Florida,* Second Edition (Sarasota, FL: Pineapple Press, 2008), 142.

Chapter 11
Page 63. "I regard that one of the essential principles..." Kelly Reynolds, *Henry Plant: Pioneer Empire Builder*, 182.

Chapter 12
Page 68. "I was born with a live oak constitution…": Edward N. Akin, *Flagler: Rockefeller Partner and Florida Baron*, 225.
Page 69. "The hopes of the people of Key West…": Martin, Sidney Walter, *Florida's Flagler*, 204.
Page 70. "There isn't enough fill…": Seth H. Bramson, *Florida East Coast Railway*, Images of America (Charleston, S. C.: Arcadia Publishing, 2006), 9
Page 71. "Flagler, you need a guardian." Sidney Walter Martin, *Florida's Flagler*, 208.
Page 71. "Joe, are you sure…": Seth Bramson, *Speedway to Sunshine*, 67.

Chapter 13
Page 74. "Flagler's Folly.": Dan Gallagher, *Florida's Great Ocean Railway* (Sarasota, FL: Pineapple Press, 2003), 3.
Page 74. "It is perfectly simple…": Les Standiford, *Last Train to Paradise* (New York, Crown Publishers, 2002), 88.
Page 75. "No man who cannot stand…": Seth Bramson, *Florida East Coast Railway*, 21.

Chapter 14
Page 80. "Passenger train to Key West…": Dan Gallagher, *Florida's Great Ocean Railway*, 176.
Page 81. "I thank God that from the summit…": Les Standiford, *Last Train to Paradise*, 204.
Page 81. "I cannot see the children…": Seth H. Bramson, "A Tale of Three Henrys," *The Journal of Decorative and Propaganda Arts* Florida Theme Issue, 1875-1945, no. 23: 138.
Page 81. "Now I can die happy…": Les Standiford, *Last Train to Paradise*, 205.
Page 83. "Eighth Wonder of the World.": Sidney Walter Martin, *Florida's Flagler*, 226, quoting the *Miami Herald* of January 22, 1912.

Afterword
Page 84. "best of friends.": Susan R. Braden, *The Architecture of Leisure*, 19.
Page 84. "If it wasn't for Florida…" Les Standiford, *Last Train to Paradise*, 212.

Index

(Numbers in **bold** refer to photographs.)

About the Author

Sandra Wallus Sammons moved from Pennsylvania to Florida and became fascinated with the Sunshine State's history. As an elementary school librarian in Lake County, Florida, she learned of the need for books on Florida's history on a fourth-grade reading level. She began writing biographies of fascinating Floridians. So many lived such inspirational lives. She now lives in central Florida with her husband and their black cat, Spades.

Here are some other books from Pineapple Press on related topics. For a complete catalog, visit our website at www.pineapplepress.com. Or write to Pineapple Press, P.O. Box 3889, Sarasota, Florida 34230-3889, or call (800) 746-3275.

Also by Sandra Wallus Sammons
Henry Flagler, Builder of Florida. An exciting biography about the man who changed Florida's east coast with his hotels and his railroads. Henry Morrison Flagler was already a millionaire when he first visited Florida in 1878. He came back and built railroads along the east coast so that others could more easily travel there. And he built grand hotels so that those who came had a beautiful place to stay. By 1912, he had built a railroad all the way to Key West. Ages 9–12. (hb, pb)

Marjory Stoneman Douglas and the Florida Everglades. Marjory Stoneman Douglas is called "the Grandmother of the Everglades." Read about her life from her childhood up north to her long and inspiring life in south Florida. When she arrived in Miami in 1915 she began to understand the importance of the Everglades, an area most considered a "swamp." She called attention to it in her book *Everglades: River of Grass.* During her 108 years, she was a newspaper and magazine journalist as well as a book writer. She received the Presidential Medal of Freedom for her work on the Everglades. Ages 9–12. (hb, pb)

Marjorie Kinnan Rawlings and the Florida Crackers. Marjorie Kinnan Rawlings grew up loving to write and hoping to become an author. Later she moved to Florida, where she lived out in the country at Cross Creek near an area called the Big Scrub. She met the people who lived there, the so-called Crackers. Their simple way of life fascinated her, so she wrote stories about them. One of her books, called *The Yearling,* was about a boy and his pet deer. This book won the Pulitzer Prize for fiction. Her dream of becoming a famous writer had come true. Ages 9–12. (hb, pb)

Other Young Reader Titles from Pineapple Press
Escape to the Everglades by Edwina Raffa and Annelle Rigsby. Fiction. Based on historical fact, this young adult novel tells the story of Will Cypress, a half-Seminole boy living among his mother's people during the Second Seminole War. He meets Chief Osceola and travels with him to St. Augustine. Ages 9–14. (hb)

Kidnapped in Key West by Edwina Raffa and Annelle Rigsby. Fiction. Twelve-year-old Eddie Malone is living in the Florida Keys in 1912 when suddenly his world is turned upside down. His father, a worker on Henry Flagler's Over-Sea Railroad, is thrown into jail for stealing the railroad payroll. Eddie is determined to prove his father's innocence. But then the real thieves kidnap Eddie. Can he escape? Well he ever get home? Will he be able to prove Pa's innocence? Ages 8–12. (hb)

The Treasure of Amelia Island by M.C. Finotti. Fiction. Mary Kingsley, the youngest child of former slave Ana Jai Kingsley, recounts the life-changing events of December 1813. Her family lived in La Florida, a Spanish territory under siege by Patriots who see no place for freed people of color in a new Florida. Against these mighty events, Mary decides to search for a legendary pirate treasure with her brothers. Ages 8–12. (hb)

CPSIA information can be obtained
at www.ICGtesting.com
Printed in the USA
BVOW08s1337060317

477773BV00001B/3/P